THE CITY OF PORTSMOUTH GIRLS' SCHOOL

The Award

for

Service To The School

for the

Academic Year
1999/2000

Awarded to

Georgina Cusworth

Headteacher

Also by Lisa Potts:

Behind the Smile
Thank You God: A Book of Children's Prayers

HEROES FOR A DAY

True stories of incredible bravery and risk

LISA POTTS

WITH LIZ BARR

Hodder & Stoughton
LONDON SYDNEY AUCKLAND

This book is dedicated to some very special people in my life who have truly been patient with me through some dark moments, and have watched me grow and heal into that nearly whole person again. I thank you.

First published in 2000

The right of Lisa Potts to be identified as the Author of the Work has been asserted by her in accordance with the Copyright, Designs and Patents Act 1988.

10 9 8 7 6 5 4 3 2 1

British Library Cataloguing in Publication Data
A record for this book is available from the British Library

ISBN 0 340 74586 X

Typeset by Avon Dataset Ltd, Bidford-on-Avon, Warks

Printed and bound in Great Britain by
The Guernsey Press Co. Ltd, Channel Isles

Hodder & Stoughton
A Division of Hodder Headline Ltd
338 Euston Road
London NW1 3BH

Contents

Acknowledgments   vii
Introduction   1
1 David Hurst QCB – The Blind Adventurer   11
2 Katharine Wells – And the Runaway Coach   29
3 Arthur Withey – 'Have-a-go' Pensioner   53
4 Daniel Gallimore – Dare to be a Daniel?   73
5 Karen and Darren Howells – The Good Neighbours   97
6 Graham Dennett – The 'Pinball Wizard'   123
7 Maria Partridge – Wheels on Fire!   141
8 Graham Roberts – The Reluctant Hero   159
9 Mary Blake – Dunblane Primary School   181
10 Euan Duncan – Unsung Hero of Everest   203

Acknowledgments

I would like to take this opportunity to say a huge thank you to the following people for making this book possible.

To all the wonderful people whose stories feature in my book, thank you for opening up to me. I know for some of you it was rather difficult. Thank you once again to Judith Longman and Charles Nettleton at Hodder for believing in this book. Thank you to Liz Barr for all her hard work on the book, the laughter and food we have shared together; oh yes, and for all the great advice! Thank you so much to Diane Hinds for all her hard work behind the scenes. Thank you to Bert Massie at RADAR for putting me in touch with different people.

I would also like to thank the following people for their great support and encouragement in my personal life.

Thank you to my dear and special parents, for their unconditional love, my fantastic brother Lee and his girlfriend Helen, and my wise and dear Aunty Pam.

Thank you to those great friends in my life – both old and new – who never let me down. I don't know where I would be without you all.

Thank you, God, for always being by my side no matter where I go or who I meet. Thank you for letting me realise some of the great gifts you have given me over the last few years.

Thank you to Peter Creagh for all the interesting lessons at college over the last two years, which has helped me to move forward immensely. Thank you once again to Phil Smith for helping me believe in myself.

Oh, and I really cannot forget that rather tall character I met on the train, whose amazing sense of humour and great strength have made us soul mates.

Introduction

The first thing to say is, what is a hero? Sometimes people call their favourite footballer or pop star their 'hero'. These are people who you probably think are great; they are your idols, but they aren't true heroes.

Then there are the people who love adventure – people who go in for dangerous sports or make expeditions to test themselves to the limit against the elements for excitement and to get themselves into the record books. And there are the crusaders – people in search of honour and glory. They are often very physically daring – but they still aren't what I mean by a true hero.

People who endure long and painful illness or physical handicaps have huge courage. This is terribly important and requires great strength of character. They are really brave, and probably to their friends and family they are the true heroes. But they aren't the kind of heroes I mean in the title of this book.

I think a hero is a person who instinctively go-gets in the face of danger, who thinks quickly and calmly and reacts fast in an emergency, and who will try their best to save the day. Finding themselves unexpectedly in a situation – sometimes a matter of life or death, sometimes just a moment of realising that they must do something quickly, because if they don't, nobody else will – the heroes of my book are all people who said, 'OK. It has to be me.'

I wanted to write this book first of all because ever since my own brush with death in 1996, I've met so many brave men and women who I would call true heroes. I had already met them all at various award ceremonies before I wrote to ask them if they would tell me their stories in their own words for my book, and that is what I've really enjoyed. I wasn't going out like an investigative journalist to do the research with strangers. I've been talking to people I know, and bringing in my own experience, because they are all people who have gone through things that I can relate to.

The second reason for writing the book is that doing it has helped me to feel better myself. I've been learning how ten very different heroes and heroines have each coped not just with their particular incident itself, but with all the things that come after. Any brush with danger or death leaves psychological as well as physical scars. Then there is learning to cope with the sudden 'fame', when you find the media outside your door every morning. Finally, there are the award ceremonies, when you are publicly called 'a hero'. Although these are always wonderful events, and you meet all sorts of famous people, for some of us this is almost the most frightening part of the whole ordeal!

It has helped me a lot to listen to how the others have each felt about all these things, and I hope that talking to me may have helped some of them as well. I know only too well how easy it is to lock away all your feelings and sit on everything. I did it for two years. It's hard to talk about some things to people who weren't there, however much you love them. But in the end it is better if you can unlock your feelings and go over it all with someone who understands, even if it means reliving it to a certain extent. I think the heroes in my book all felt that I understood at least part of what they had experienced, and I hope it helped them a bit to open up about it. I know for me that it has been a really big part of my healing process.

Even now I sometimes think, 'Am I a heroine?' I know what I did that day, but like so many of the people in this book, I feel detached from it. I sometimes feel as though I'm talking about somebody else. When I think about their stories, I see the other people in this book more as heroes and heroines than I see myself as one. And I think they all feel the same way.

I've told the story of what happened to me in my book, *Behind the Smile*, but in case you haven't read that, or can't remember exactly what did happen on Monday 8 July 1996, I'll tell you now, as briefly as I can. It's impossible to tell it very quickly, because although I now know that the whole attack can only have taken a few minutes, at the time it felt like hours and hours.

When I woke up that morning, it was just like any other day. I chatted to my mum over breakfast and gave her a kiss and hug when I left for work. I drove off to St Luke's Infants School with my teddy sitting on the passenger seat next to me, because that afternoon we were having a teddy bears' picnic. It was for the nursery class children and for some of the little ones who were due to start at the nursery the following September.

Dorothy Hawes, the nursery class teacher, and I prepared all the picnic things, blew up balloons and prepared face paints. The children were all so excited that afternoon when they ran in with their teddy bears. One little boy, Ahmed, was having his first visit to the nursery, to see what it was going to be like when he started the next September. He didn't speak much English, and his mum came up to me and asked, 'Will he be all right?' I assured her that he would have a great time. That short sentence will never leave my mind. Soon I would be carrying around the guilt that this little boy was going to be scarred for the rest of his life.

Some of the mums came to help that afternoon. The children had their faces painted like little teddy bears and two of them were pandas, with black and white faces and whiskers. At the picnic we sat the children down around the tablecloth with their teddies on their laps. We passed round sandwiches, crisps, teddy bear biscuits and chocolates, and then I went inside to make drinks for the parents.

I took the drinks out to the mums, who were standing against the nursery fence. We talked about the lovely weather and I said, 'Only a week left of term and then you'll have the children under your feet for six weeks.' They were all laughing. One of the mums said, 'Let's have a photo of you, Miss Potts.'

A little while later one of the children asked me to go to the field with them, and they pulled me onto the small grass area where we started to play ring-a-ring o' roses with the teddy bears. There were about eight children with me; the rest were playing with skipping ropes and balls.

Dorothy called over to me to ask the time and I said, 'Gosh, it's 3.12!' I remember thinking how quickly the time had gone. Dorothy called, 'Come on then, children, time to pack away now. Put the balls and skipping ropes in the basket and then line up against the wall.' Some of the children went to line up straight away and others were still running around on the grass. I started to collect up skipping ropes and balls, and I was showing one little girl,

4

Francesca, how to fold the ropes up properly so they wouldn't get in a knot.

I heard Dorothy say, 'Hello, how are you?' I turned round to see that she was speaking to Wendy Willington, one of the mums, who was walking on the infants field, the other side of the three-foot fence, on her way to pick up her son from the infants school. I said 'hello' to her too and as I turned back I saw, out of the corner of my eye, a man running round the side of the school building. He was tall and black and he was wearing a trilby hat. A grey bag was slung across his chest and in his right hand he was carrying a large knife.

It looked like a plastic toy because it had no shine on it. I heard Dorothy say, 'Quick, run inside,' and she shepherded some of the children into the nursery. In another second the man had lifted the knife above his head and smashed it straight down onto Wendy Willington's head. I saw her shopping bag fall to the ground, and then she fell too. There was blood everywhere.

Suddenly there was complete chaos and panic. The children were screaming, the parents were screaming, but somehow I felt very calm. I grabbed some of the children in my arms and turned to run them into the nursery school. As I spun round, I saw the man bring his knife down on the head of Surinda, Reena's mum. Surinda half-turned as if to run, then collapsed. Then he did the same to Fatama's mum.

I felt my long skirt rise up as children gathered underneath it, screaming my name.

The man leapt across the fence. I ran with the children towards the nursery door, pushing and shoving them inside. I saw Dorothy about ten feet inside the nursery, and remember thinking that she had a lot of the children with her, but that there must be some still left outside. So I knew I had to go back.

As I turned to run back for more children, the man's face was right up against mine. I lifted both my hands to shield my face and watched this huge blade strike – almost in slow motion – down into my left arm. My left hand was nearly severed, but I didn't feel any pain, just a feeling of wetness on my cardigan.

I started grabbing some of the children and pushing them inside. The man lifted the knife again to strike Francesca, who was holding on to my skirt. It looked as if he was aiming for her neck, so I flung out my hand to protect her. As the knife came down, my hand went up, but the knife skimmed above my hand and straight across her face. The whole of her left cheek was ripped apart. I looked into her eyes – they were totally glazed.

The man turned round and began running round the playground brandishing his knife. I ran a couple more children to the nursery door and shoved them through, then spun around again and saw that little Ahmed and his sister Marium were still outside. For a fraction of a second I did think, 'What am I going to do?' But I knew immediately there was no way I could leave the two of them alone outside. As I ran back, Marium ran full force into me, screaming, 'My brother, my brother!' Three-year-old Ahmed was running after her, with the man chasing them both. Then Ahmed fell. The man was right behind him with the knife raised. I ran to pick Ahmed up, although I have no idea how I lifted him, because my left hand was hanging loose. It has to be a miracle. But even as I picked him up the man sliced across his head. I put my right hand in the way, but the same slice that cut Ahmed's head open also ripped open my hand. I saw a lot of blood and Ahmed became very quiet.

I got inside with the children and tried to pull the door shut, but it wouldn't shut. The man's foot was in the door. The door to the reception class was to the side of us. I thought we could run through there and into the main school building. The man was right behind me as I reached out to open the reception class door, but just as I tried to turn the handle, I suddenly knew I couldn't go that way. There were about twenty-five terrified little children in the classroom, and all their lives would be in danger if I opened the door and the man followed us in. Their teacher, Linda, was holding the door shut against me – the hardest thing she has ever had to do in her life.

Too late, I realised that we should have gone the other way and run straight through the nursery. Now we were trapped. We were in a very small area with the man behind us, the closed reception class door in front, a dressing-up trolley on one side and some cupboards on the other side. There were six or seven children trapped with me. They were all screaming and I was frantic. The piercing screams of the children will never ever leave me.

I put the unconscious Ahmed down on the floor at the side of the dressing-up trolley where he could be hidden with clothes. I gathered all the other children in front of me and protected them as much as I could with my own body. As I leaned over their huddled little bodies, the man brought the machete down twice on my back.

I was sure we were all going to die, and I shall never know why the man decided to turn round and go back out of the door into the playground again, but he did.

As soon as I realised he was going, I began to kick and push the children around the corner so that they could run through the nursery and out of the far door into the school's main entrance. Ahmed was still lying behind the dressing-up trolley, I could see his feet sticking out, but I just had to leave him there so I could take the other children to safety. Marium was clinging to my skirt, still screaming for her brother; Reena was under one of my arms and another child under the other. I was weighed down with children clinging to my skirt, and I had to push and shove and kick them to make them run in front of me.

As I started to run I felt another blow go down the back of my head. The man had come back. We carried on running. Right in front of us, blocking our way, was a big water tray. I will never know how we all jumped over such a huge object, especially with the two children still under my arms, and severe injuries to my hands. All I know is that we made it.

I didn't see the man again until I had to face him in court five months later.

Writing my story for my book a year after the event did help me begin to sort out some of my feelings about what happened that day, and about what happened afterwards, right up to the day in 1997 when I got the George Medal from the Queen. But mostly for those first two years I felt as though I was on a merry-go-round. Other people took charge of my life and I just rode along, up and down, round and round. So many different things were happening to me, and I seemed to be always doing what other people were asking me to do, going where I was asked to go, giving interviews, being photographed, trying to tell the story over and over again. And yet I felt strangely detached from it. A lot of my own real feelings about it all were still quite suppressed, pushed down inside me. Friends wanted me to talk to them, but I found I didn't want to.

That was right up to September 1998, when I went into hospital for further operations on my left arm. For the first time in ages I had a few weeks just to myself, to think and be quiet, and that was when I really started to cry. And I think that was when I started to recover. That was when I started planning this book. I realised that talking to other people about their experiences would help me. So working on this has been a big part of my healing process, to get me back to being that whole person. I know I'm still not quite there, but I'm on the way.

It's been great fun to do as well. Just to be with some of these people and really listen to what they did and how they dealt with it, not from reading about it in the papers but in their own words. Not all the stories are as dreadful as mine. Some of them are even quite funny, and I definitely found that a good sense of humour turns out to be an essential quality for a hero!

I asked all of them whether or not they believed in God. I have a strong faith. I believe that God was with me – and the children – on that day and shared everything we went through. I would never want to say to anyone else that they should believe in God, because I think people get their strength in all sorts of ways. If they want to look for God, they will. But I was interested to know whether or not faith had had anything to do with the way the people in my book had reacted on their own day of facing danger.

These stories are all about heroes, whatever they have done, whether it's a big or a small thing. They have all dealt with things differently. For some of them it's all forgotten and they couldn't think what all the fuss was about. For some of them it will be a story they will tell their grandchildren in years to come, and get out the old press cuttings and *999 Lifesavers* videos and have a good laugh. But I think an important thing is that for many of them, as for me, it will have changed their lives forever. It isn't like in the movies: where the hero or heroine gets in a fight, or gets shot, and then gets straight up again and carries on as though nothing has happened. It is truly about pain and suffering for a long time afterwards – a lot of pain and suffering.

I can identify with every single one of the stories in this book. Obviously I can't always go the whole journey, because each one is completely different, but I can identify with a lot of their feelings. Mainly, I think, I identify with Mary in Dunblane, because our situation was so similar. I could go further on the journey with her than with anyone.

When you read their stories, you will see that none of my heroes or heroines expected to hit the headlines. None of them were out looking for some special excitement. They are all ordinary people, just like you and me, who suddenly found that in a crisis they were able to keep their heads and save the day. These people have all done it, and they are just a small sample. So tomorrow, if something happens to any of us, or to our children, we can hope, because of what my heroes all did, that someone else will be a hero for that day.

1

David Hurst QCB – The Blind Adventurer

A Sea Rescue

29 July 1997

I met Dave at the Unsung Heroes Award at the Dorchester Hotel in 1997. I had received this award in 1996, but the following year they had decided to invite back some of the past winners, to make it a special evening to celebrate the twenty years of rewarding Unsung Heroes.

I was sitting all ready to go with my mum, in reception at the hotel where we were staying, waiting for the minibus that would take us to the Dorchester for the ceremony. And Dave was also sitting there, chatting away to his wife, and they seemed really nice, so I introduced myself. I said, 'Hello, I'm Lisa. I'm going along to this award ceremony, are you?'

Dave exclaimed, '*You're* Lisa!' and he reached out and touched me, because he was blind, so he couldn't see me. And we just hit it off straight away. Dave was very friendly and he's a real character. He told my mum that he and his wife, Penny, had followed my story and that they had been so excited knowing that they were going to meet me. That sounded really funny to me, because I'm just me.

We went on chatting all the way to the Dorchester in the minibus. We sat together at the dinner table and all the time we never stopped talking and laughing. I thought he was a great guy, and Penny, his wife, was lovely. We've kept in touch since that evening.

Dave told me about some of the amazing things that he had done since he went blind in 1981, when he was in his mid-twenties. He got his Unsung Heroes award about ten years ago, for all the charity work that he'd done that had made him dubbed in the press as 'the blind adventurer'. He ran thirty-three marathons and twelve half-marathons in three years and raised over a million pounds. He was the first blind person to walk the Pennine Way. He was the leader on a survival expedition through the jungles of Borneo.

On his second attempt he became the first blind man to climb Mont Blanc in France. He just failed to reach the summit of Mount McKinley in Alaska a few feet from the summit, due to adverse weather conditions. He has also climbed Mount Kinabaloo, the highest peak in South East Asia.

He has won three gold medals for Great Britain for blind water-skiing in Australia, and holds the world record for blind water-ski jumping at 14 metres. He represented Great Britain at the Paralympics in Seoul and won the silver medal in blind judo.

But although all of this is amazing, and he's a really brave and determined person, he's also very funny about it. He's not serious for a moment. He gave a speech at these Unsung Heroes Awards, and the whole audience was in stitches. Often people's stories are sad and make you cry, but not Dave's. Not at all. And also – in case you are thinking I'm going back on what I said in the introduction about heroes – it was not for any of these things I've just mentioned that I asked him to be one of the 'heroes' in my book.

In 1993 Dave injured his neck in a judo competition which forced him to retire from competitive sport. He continued to do his charity work, particularly in the field of helping disabled people come to terms with their disability, but by then he had married Penny, and their son, Aaron David, had been born in 1991. By early 1997 Dave and Penny decided that he'd had enough adventures, enough limelight and the pressure of living in a town where everyone knew him, and all these challenging things he'd done had begun to tire him out. He wanted to spend more time at home with Penny and Aaron. So they moved from Stockport to a remote little village called Borth by the Irish Sea in West Wales, in search of a quiet life. But then, a little over a week after they had moved in, David found himself in the headlines again – after rescuing someone from the sea. And that is his story for my book.

I went to see Dave and Penny in their cottage at Borth, and as we walked along the lovely four-and-a-half-mile stretch of clean, sandy beach, arm in arm on a beautiful sunny day, Dave told me his story.

Dave's Story

We live directly opposite the beach in a little cottage believed to be about three hundred years old, made from beams from old sailing ships in the roof timbers, and things like that. It was one of the original properties before the rest of the village was built.

On 29 July 1997 we had moved into the house less than a fortnight before. We were still doing a bit of the unpacking of the endless boxes. It was a lovely day. I decided that my little boy Aaron and I should go out swimming. Aaron is almost eight now, so he was six at the time. We go swimming quite often because it's lovely to have the sea just across the road.

We went across to the beach – Aaron with his bucket and spade and his body board. It was mid-afternoon. The tide was on the turn from going out to coming back in. It was a beautiful day, but there was a leading edge of a storm coming in – so I suppose the waves would have been 1.5 to 2 metres high, with really good surf. After a while I left Aaron building a sandcastle on the beach and asked a couple who were there with their two children to keep an eye on him while I went out for a swim.

There were quite a lot of people in the water; children in dinghies, and on airbeds and things like that. It's amazing to me how many children go out there. Parents don't seem to realise how dangerous it is. The wind can be very strong here, so it can easily blow them out to sea, or off down towards the estuary.

I was swimming out – I suppose about 60 to 100 metres offshore, because round here it shelves off very, very slowly, and you have to go out a long way before you are out of your depth. It's very hard to say and to this day I don't know exactly how far out I was. When I do go swimming I always go quite a distance out so that airbeds and low flying dinghies are not attacking me. I'm a strong swimmer. I was never a quick swimmer, but I have always been able to swim for miles and miles and miles.

I heard this faint voice shouting for help. I thought it was probably a child on an airbed being pulled out to sea. It was an awful situation, because of course I couldn't see them, I could only hear them calling for help. They sounded quite a bit away, but it's very difficult to tell, because the wind can make it sound nearer or further away. The waves were getting bigger because the wind was getting up, so I was having to swim through them rather than over them.

I heard them shouting again, 'I can't get back in.'

I remember thinking, 'Do I go back to the beach? But how do I find the right person among the thousands on the beach, and explain to them what's happening out here?' Because I wouldn't be able to point to them, and by then they could have drifted even further out. At this point I was still sure it was a child on an airbed, who I thought would be frightened if I swam away and left them.

I wasn't at all concerned about my own safety. I've done white-water rafting on some very big rivers out in the Yukon, and in Alaska, so the open sea doesn't hold many terrors for me.

I decided I must try and help. I shouted, 'If you keep calling out, I'll swim over to you.'

I just had to think to myself about the direction of the wind. The one thing is, if you can't see, you are used to the unknown happening and unexpected things coming upon you, because they do that every day of your life. Some people think it's clever to be able to think, if the wind is blowing left to right, and I'm on the left of him, and he's shouting, he'll sound further to the right than he is, because the wind is carrying his voice away. But it was quite natural to me. If you are blind, you do it all the time, because when you cross a road, a car can sound nearer or further away according to the wind.

I knew from where they sounded that I needed to head further off to the left, if you are facing the beach. I knew I could get somewhere near them, but if the wind was blowing hard they could be even further left, but would sound nearer.

So I swam along and as I got nearer, I discovered that it wasn't a child; it was a young man with a surfboard, and he must have tired himself out, trying and failing to surf back to the beach. Borth beach is a popular place for surfers. Prince Charles came surfing here in his early days as Prince of Wales.

So I was chatting away all the time I was swimming towards him, 'It's really interesting out here today, isn't it? The waves are really quite big for surfing.' Just saying whatever came into my head, because the last thing I wanted was for him to know that I couldn't see. I didn't want him to start panicking or think that he'd got to rescue some poor blind bloke. So it was one of these ironic situations where, if you like, which is worse? Somebody out there who isn't a strong swimmer, who didn't know what to do, but who could see, or somebody who couldn't see, but did know what to do, and knew they were a strong enough swimmer to cope with the situation?

When I reached him I found he was in the water, hanging on to his surfboard. I held on beside him and we had a rather strange conversation.

He said to me, 'How deep is it?'

I said, 'Well, I'm not diving down to look. If you're that interested you can go and look!'

He was in his mid to late twenties and he'd hired a surfboard for the first time and fallen under the misapprehension that a lot of people do, that you just have to point it at the beach and it will bring you back in. I told him that it doesn't work that way. You have to know how to catch the waves, and how to choose the right wave that will take you all the way in.

So I started to swim back to shore, pulling the surfboard along behind me, with this man holding on to it. I couldn't tell if he could swim or not, but he'd obviously tired himself out and was all in. He had hired a board and he had it fastened round his leg, so he wouldn't lose it. I think he thought that as long as he stayed with it, he was going to float.

He said, 'The tide would have eventually washed me back in, wouldn't it?'

I said, 'Well, it might have done, but after how long? And where? You just don't know.'

I was thinking to myself that he probably wouldn't have got in that way. It was a beautiful day, but there was a gusty offshore wind and the edge of a storm coming in. The sea was getting rough with breaking waves, and the currents were probably pulling him further and further offshore, which is why he had started to panic. But when all is said and done, there wasn't much danger in any of it. He had a surfboard, which floats. It's not as if he had been actually drowning and I had had to pull him out of the water and give him artificial respiration. All I had to do was to keep him calm and control the situation. So it was just a case of swimming back in and using the tide and the wind to help you rather than, as he had been doing, fighting against them.

I had been hoping all the time that somebody on the beach would see what was happening and would alert the coastguard. All this time I was swimming back to shore, pulling the surfboard, and he lay across it, swimming with his legs in the water. You can't swim directly back to the beach, because of the way the tide pulls you. You have to swim at an angle, coming in slowly, which is what we did. I suppose it was about 400 metres further along the beach by the time we actually got back in. I don't know how long it took, but long enough for me to be beginning to feel concerned about Aaron being on his own.

The guy didn't know I was blind until the moment we got back to the beach. That was the ironic bit. Because I needed rescuing then! There's nothing to fall over in the sea, but there is on the beach. I was in a predicament then, because I hadn't got a cane with me, so he would have to guide me back to where Aaron was on the beach.

I asked him to tell me what was round about, so that I could tell him where my little boy was. He told me what buildings were behind us and I said, 'Oh well, I want to be about four or five groins further along the beach.' He asked if I'd got salt in my eyes or something, making me unable to see. I said that no, it was just that my eyes didn't work.

From that point on, there was no more conversation. We walked along the beach in complete silence. It was really weird. It was as though he was struck dumb. He just became completely silent. I suppose it must have come as quite a shock to realise that the person who has rescued you was a blind man.

I don't know if he suddenly realised how close a shave he'd really had. I suppose he was trying to mull it all over in his mind. It must have been a million to one chance, worse than a needle in a haystack, a surfer in the Irish Sea for a blind man to find? It was pure chance that I was in the right place at the right time. I couldn't have stood on the beach, and thought, 'That looks like somebody in trouble out there.'

We got back, and a whole load of people were around, because someone had called the coastguard, who came and took our names and addresses. The coastguard said, 'We don't really recommend that people swim out to save people.' He wasn't to know how good a swimmer I was, or that I knew what to do. All I can say is that people started calling me a hero. They said, 'The sea was so rough, and you swam out there.' They didn't know I was blind. Nobody knew I was blind on the beach, except for the man I was standing next to and my little boy, Aaron – and he didn't snitch.

People were saying all the usual sort of things, 'How marvellous.'

I said, 'Anybody would have done it.'

They said, 'If that was the case, there would have been thousands of people in the sea and nobody on the beach.'

You don't look at it like that. At the time you just do what has to be done. It just happens. In some ways it was almost as though someone else had taken control of your actions. You go into automatic. I know I just acted from instinct.

I was more concerned that Aaron was all right, because I'd been a lot longer than he would have expected. He was quite happy when I got back, making sand pies. Penny was there, too, sitting on the sea wall, being nosy with the next-door neighbours, seeing what was going on. Penny told me that she had been upstairs in the bedroom watching the crowd gathering, and wondering what was happening, and then suddenly realised that I was in the middle of it all. So she had come down and spoken to the coastguard.

I wasn't in shock or anything. I was just mentally exhausted. It had been quite hard work to swim out and swim back in, because it wasn't just a short distance. People often ask, 'How far was it?' Or 'How long did it take?' I haven't got a clue. All I know is, swimming over there regularly now, and realising how far out I have to swim to be out of my depth, we must have been quite some distance.

Somebody had said to Penny, 'He's just saved somebody. He's just saved a surfer.'

So when she saw me she said, 'Now what have you been up to?' I thought I'd have to go to my bed without any tea!

It was at that point that I realised how incredibly stupid what I'd done had been. The sane thing would have been to swim back to shore and get help. But I honestly believed at first that it was a child, and that I couldn't just leave them. You see plenty of young children getting into trouble on airbeds. Only a week later a young girl of nine further down the coast was drowned. I felt so sad that she wasn't as lucky, that somebody wasn't there, or something didn't happen to save her. Parents who bring children to the seaside for holidays don't realise how dangerous it is, when it looks so beautiful, and the children are out swimming or in dinghies or on airbeds. If they actually realised how dangerous it was they certainly wouldn't be sleeping on the beach while their children were in the water.

That's why whenever Aaron is swimming, I always go and swim with him. Then, if I want to swim afterwards, he can do sandcastles. I suppose in a sense that leaving Aaron alone on the beach to build sandcastles is a bit on the dangerous side too, these days. But the beach is almost our front garden, we're living so close to it. And of course, I use Aaron as my guide when I'm walking across to the beach. I'm afraid that children who have disabled parents often grow up a lot faster than they should do.

Anyway, that afternoon, when the coastguard had gone I realised I was quite tired. I honestly thought at that point that Penny, Aaron and I would go home, and that would be it. The whole thing would just blow over. I didn't think it was any big deal. All I'd done was swim in with a guy on a surfboard. That was *all* I did. It wasn't as though he was drowning or anything. He was just being taken out to sea, and had grown tired. That was all it was.

But then of course the newspapers got hold of it . . . and went bananas.

When we got in I went for a shower, and I remember Peter from next door coming in. He's a real wind-up merchant, so I thought he was joking when he said, 'The press will be coming onto you any minute now.'

I said to him, 'Oh, yes! Well, tell me why?'

He said, 'You're blind, and you went out in a high sea and saved that surfer.'

I said, 'Well, that's no reason for the press to come on.'

You go through your life, and there are people and events that make a dramatic change in your life, such a dramatic change in your life. I suppose I am thinking of how such terrible things have happened to children, like the little girl only a week later who drowned, like the children at Dunblane, and of course the little ones at your school. Who wouldn't try and save them if they could?

Only one person could ever answer my own question about heroism and that is you, Lisa. Why did you go out twice? I remember thinking to myself at the time that I could well understand why Lisa grabbed some children and ran in, but I could never understand why you went out again and again. I don't honestly know whether I would have gone out again. A lot of people must have asked themselves what they would have done, but you can't answer that unless you are in that situation.

If somebody had said to you, 'Right, during your training as a nursery nurse, we're going to put together a scenario. You are out in the garden with forty children having a party. Somebody rushes up and starts stabbing them and lashing out at the children . . . What would you do?'

I think probably everybody would say, 'I haven't got a clue. Run, probably. Or just stand there, completely shocked.' But when it came to it – you didn't.

But now people were calling *me* a hero for doing such a little thing. I said, 'I don't consider myself a hero, I didn't have a choice in what I did, because it just happened.'

The *Daily Mail* rang that evening. They interviewed me over the telephone. It appeared in the paper a day or two later, because first of all they sent an intrepid photographer down to wild Wales! And then of course, when it comes out in one paper, it goes absolutely bananas. All the papers, Sky Television, HTV, the radio stations were on to me. We still have the cuttings, but I can't remember what they say. We collect the cuttings, but I don't think it's ever to look at them again. It's more just for your children and grandchildren.

And then it went out in the United States in their news programmes. It really is that quirky – I don't think if I'd been sighted there would have been anything like the press coverage.

I think with all the expeditions I've done in the past, and life-saving and all of that, it was just part and parcel of how I've always lived my life since I went blind twenty years ago. At the time when I first lost my sight, I was working with people with profound and multiple handicaps. I had spent all my working life telling them that they can overcome things. So when the shoe was on the other foot, I remember thinking, 'I can't let them down, by not coping myself. What sort of effect would it have on their lives if something happens to Dave and he doesn't cope?' It puts you under an awful lot of pressure. I did begin by feeling sorry for myself. I remember, at first, sitting at home not doing anything very much, and then suddenly thinking, did I really want to spend the rest of my life, from being in my mid-twenties, sat in a chair doing nothing? There had to be more to life.

But anyway, after this swimming incident, there was the usual week's flurry of newspaper and radio and television interviews. Then it all died down for a bit. Then the Queen's Commendation for Bravery Award came through, and there was another resurgence of press attention.

After our long walk on the beach Dave and I went back into the cottage for tea, and Penny told me how she felt about it all. First she told me how she had actually spoken to the man Dave had rescued.

Penny: Nobody round here ever heard from Patrick Flack, the lad Dave had saved, again. It was a great mystery. I spoke to him very briefly when Dave was talking to the coastguard. I asked Patrick what had happened and he said he'd had a struggle, that he'd got stuck out at sea on a surfboard and David had swam out and helped him get back in. Then he went off, never to be seen again.

We don't know where he came from or where he went. He gave his address to the coastguard as the Seabank Hotel, Aberystwyth. It was more a hostel than a holiday hotel, and has burned down since. But he never returned to it after the incident. And he's never been seen since.

The press hounded him, and hounded and hounded. They waited outside the Seabank Hotel for months afterwards. Where did Patrick Flack go? It's one of the 'Great Mysteries of Aberystwyth' – according to the *Cambria News!*

Dave: I should imagine he just didn't want any publicity. It wouldn't surprise me. He'd gone out surfing in conditions that were really too rough for a first-time surfer. He'd made a miscalculation and having been lucky enough to get away with it, he must have considered that the last thing he wanted was to have his face plastered all over the newspapers. And I can quite understand that. You would just want to melt into the background.

Lisa: Penny, do you think Dave was a hero?

Penny: I just see Dave as Dave. It was just such a typical thing for him to do. At first it didn't seem anything special. I thought he had been brave, but it was what I would have expected of him. No, I didn't think he was 'a hero'.

That evening we sat at the dinner table and he just chatted away about what had happened. I was a bit amazed.

I think he was pretty surprised at himself. Aaron was very excited that his daddy had done this. But having been married to Dave for eight or nine years at that point, I was pretty used to it.

Then soon after that we had everybody here. The *Daily Mail*. Dave was on Sky Television, HTV. . . It was a bit like being back in Stockport again, because that was what it was like there all the time. Everybody knew him there and what he had done. He was always being interviewed.

It was more extraordinary for our little boy. He wasn't used to it. Obviously we enjoyed all the attention. And Aaron definitely did. He thought he was in heaven.

And then there was the award. First of all the lifeboat people, the coastguards, sent a commemorative plaque. It's downstairs on the wall. That was a sort of 'thank you' for doing it, and they sent a really nice letter as well.

Then the Queen's Commendation for Bravery came through. It was one of these registered letters that you have to sign for. We hadn't ordered anything, so I had no idea what it could be. It said this award would be announced in the *London Gazette* in a couple of days' time. We were to tell nobody. Would Dave let them know if he was prepared to accept it? We were both gobsmacked, because we hadn't got a clue what it was.

We didn't go to Buckingham Palace. The presentation was done here in Wales, by the Lord Lieutenant of Dyfed, representing the Queen. Dave's mum was there, and my mum. Neighbours from either side of the cottage came along. And our butcher!

I was so proud that day. It was a lovely day. It wasn't over the top or anything, just a few speeches and then the presentation. There was a wonderful buffet where everyone could chat to each other. The Lord Lieutenant was very relaxed and he talked to the children, who played with his sword.

Dave: You feel incredibly honoured, but you don't think you deserve it. You get carried along in this wake, in the aftermath of whatever happened and you just want somebody to stop it and let you get off the roundabout. Because all these accolades get put on you, but you don't feel they are deserved. You just consider that you were incredibly fortunate to have been in the right place at the right time, and to have been able to help someone.

I think these things that happen make you realise how precious life is. And how there's such a small dividing line between living and dying. I think you said at that Unsung Heroes evening that despite all the medals and all the awards – to see those children's smiling faces, that's the real reward. They may still have problems getting over it, but at least their mothers and fathers still have sons and daughters. And that's exactly how I feel.

I think it might make me feel very proud to know that there is a life going on somewhere that might not have been. To follow the generations. I sometimes wonder whether, maybe in two or three years' time, when he's married and has children, that guy may think that perhaps those children of his are there because of what happened. You never know.

But I also think about what would have happened to my family and friends if it had all turned out differently and, as the coastguard said, we had ended up with two fatalities. It's like a moment in history, everything follows on from that. I don't know whether that explains it, but I do have very mixed feelings.

I believe that there is something that is far more powerful than we are, and whether it's God or Allah, or whatever name you call it, I believe that things happen throughout your life that have meaning because of this power. I'm not a churchgoer but I do believe that most things happen for a reason. I find it hard to believe that you can be 'chosen' to have an adverse thing, like going blind. But even that changes your life, and it may be for the better.

Everybody's life has ups and downs and the important thing is to do what you can and what you believe is right. I liken it to a race and I often say, was it the person who came last in the race that failed? Or was it the person who never took part? If in a marathon you run three steps, then you have achieved three steps – you haven't failed because you didn't run twenty-six miles.

During dramatic times in your life, there is always a light at the end of the tunnel. It might seem a heck of a long way and a long time coming, but if you can just hang on in there, once you've hit the bottom, there is only the way up.

Lisa's Reflections

I've felt really close to Dave ever since I first met him. A lot of what he says makes great sense to me. When he said he thought the whole thing would just blow over, he'd go home and that would be it – that is exactly what I thought about my own incident. Even when I went to interview Dave, a year after his incident had happened, the next day the BBC were coming to his house to film a reconstruction of the whole thing for *999 Lifesavers*.

I don't think anyone who hasn't been through it can know what a shock all the media attention is. I remember how I couldn't believe that the next day all of a sudden there were all these people wanting to talk to me. Then I thought, 'OK, it's news. They'll talk to me, and then after a week it will all be over.' What I didn't realise was that a year, two, three, nearly four years on, people would still be asking me the same questions. People ask me about it constantly. Really they are asking themselves 'Would I have done that?' Unfortunately or fortunately I was the one put in that situation that day, or I could be one of the people still asking myself the question. I just thank God that I did what I did that day. And even I don't know what I would do on another day.

Dave asked me why I had kept going back out for more children. I think he answered that question himself, when he said that at the time of the incident, it was almost as though somebody else was in control. He said he thought I might understand that better than anybody. It is something I hadn't really thought about until I did this interview with Dave. But he's right. It *was* as though it was somebody else. I knew it was me, but it was as though the power to act was coming from somewhere else. Almost like I was out of my body, or in a dream. As though it was something I could never have done in real life. That adrenaline kicks in and takes over your body.

Everyone knows Dave in Borth now. When I went out with him on the street, everyone was shouting, 'Hello, Dave!' He's a very brave, laughing man who everyone likes, who after he'd gone blind just thought, 'No, forget this' and got up and did all those mad things like climbing mountains. You wonder why – because when he reaches the summit, he can't see – but he seems to get all sorts of different things out of each experience. It takes a certain kind of person to pull their life back together after going blind, who can say, 'This has happened, and I've got to deal with it.'

There's a very deep side to him, too. He talked to me about how he would never see his son. I said, 'Oh, that's so sad. It must be awful.'

He said, 'No, it isn't awful. You get given another sense. You can feel people's emotions more, you can sense their moods almost better when you can't see their face.'

With all the interviews I did for this book, all of them have been very positive people, and all of them have got great strength of character. I think that shows very much with Dave. I think he's great. Although he's very modest about what he did, he did save another person's life. He laughs it off and talks about it like it is nothing, but I think everyone knows how dangerous the sea can be. An exhausted man clinging on to a surfboard out at sea wouldn't have stood much of a chance on his own.

2

Katharine Wells –
And the Runaway Coach

Winchester Bypass

1 April 1996

Katharine and I first met at the People of the Year Awards, which is where I met quite a few of the people in this book. RADAR, the Royal Association for Disability and Rehabilitation, give these awards every year in November. It's been going for years and years. It used to be Men of the Year. Then they changed it to People of the Year.

Katharine was one of the People of the Year in November 1996, the same year as me. She had prevented the coach she was travelling in from causing a multiple collision on the motorway when the driver collapsed.

I think because we were the two youngest girls there, she came up to me and we started chatting. Her twin brothers were with her, and her mum, and they were all really sweet. I had taken my cousin with me, so we all sat together and had a good giggle and a laugh. I liked

Katharine immediately, and she struck me as having a very good sense of humour, and of being a great character in her own right.

I think because we were two young girls and sitting at the same table, they picked Katharine and me, along with the head teacher from Dunblane, to be photographed together that year.

My interview with Katharine for this book took place three years later, when we met in a café one lunchtime, in London's Oxford Street. After a formal start, it turned into just two girls chatting over coffee more than an interview, so I've left in quite a bit of my side of the conversation as Katharine told me the full story of the runaway coach.

Katharine's Story

My name is Katharine Wells. I was born on 20 February 1975. I now live in London, but in 1996 I lived with my mum and brothers at home in Bournemouth. I have a diploma in leisure and tourism and at that time I was working for National Express.

I was a coach stewardess, which means greeting the passengers, collecting tickets, and all the general customer services. An average day for me would be to meet the coach at the bus depot first thing in the morning, drive to Poole, pick up passengers from Poole, then drive back to Bournemouth, pick up more passengers, drive to Ringwood and pick up more passengers. And then it was onwards to London. Usually the journey to London took two-and-a-half hours and during that time I would serve snacks and refreshments.

We'd stop off at Heathrow where we would drop off passengers for the airport and pick up others for central London. The London destination was Victoria. We would stay there for forty minutes and then, with different passengers on board, drive back, and do the same thing on the way back, picking up and dropping off passengers on the way.

Lisa: *What happened on 1 April, the day of the incident?*

Katharine: Well, it was bizarre, because I was actually preparing myself for an interview the next day with Virgin Atlantic as an air stewardess. For two weeks prior to that day I had been concentrating so hard on that, going down to the gym, getting my beauty sleep, eating healthily, and I had my mind totally focussed on this job interview. And that particular day, it was so funny because I had a nail appointment, so that . . .

Lisa: *Sorry. Did you say 'inhalant'?*

Katharine: *Nail* appointment! To have my nails extended. So my main focus for that day was finishing work and then driving straight to my nail appointment as soon as we got back from London. Anyway, in the morning we had just left Ringwood, and we were on the way to London. I was doing my rounds, taking orders and getting refreshments, making teas and coffees and whatnot. It was a packed coach. It was the first day of the Easter school holidays. There were forty-six people on the coach – forty-four passengers, the driver and myself.

I was in the galley area at the back of the coach as we were nearing Winchester, on the Winchester bypass, a brand new section of motorway that'd been opened up fairly recently. There had been a lot of controversy about that, because they had to cut through the countryside to build the road. The road dips, it goes right down and then it comes up. We were rolling down the hill. I was at the back of the coach getting my orders ready – it seems funny now, to think about it.

The coach suddenly started veering left and right, so I came out from the back where I was making up sandwiches, to find out what was going on. A couple of people at the front started screaming. My initial thought was that maybe we were being cut up or something by another driver, and being forced off the road. I didn't have any idea of what was going to happen. I just started walking forward to see what was happening. Then I saw that the driver was slumped over the steering wheel. So then I dashed to the front.

I didn't know the driver very well because he'd been off for a long time. He'd had a heart operation, and he had only recently come back to work. It was only about the second or third time I'd worked with him since he'd got back, so I knew a lot of the other drivers far better than I knew him.

Lisa: What did you do? Did you have to move the driver? Did you have to give him a big shove?

Katharine: No! I didn't shove him – it's a big steering wheel, so I just moved him over to the side. I didn't have control of the whole steering wheel like you would normally; I literally had just the top bit . . . because he was still partly slumped over it. And then I . . .

Lisa: So you just leaned over and took the wheel? By then were there any cars on either side of the coach? Were there other drivers hooting their horns?

Katharine: I don't think I would have noticed anything like that. I was just trying to get the coach to the side of the road and brake and get the hazard lights on and things. All I could think about was stopping this coach. Stop the coach, and then as soon as the coach is stopped I'll worry about everything else. I had been shown how to use the brakes, because there is an emergency brake in the side panel. You've got your foot brakes – foot pedals – which are obviously the normal ones to use, and then you've got an emergency brake, which is like a lever, in the side panel, which stops it quite suddenly. And that was the only brake I could get to.

So I managed to steer the coach in to the side and put the emergency brake on as slowly as I could. We eventually stopped on the hard shoulder.

Lisa: Did you feel panic?

Katharine: Not until afterwards. Not until the coach had actually stopped. And then the worst thing about that was having forty-four people looking at you. Forty-four people on a coach in the middle of a motorway, wanting to know what was going on and what was going to happen to them . . . was everything going to be all right? And there was only me to answer all their questions.

Lisa: Had many people been screaming?

Katharine: Only the four people who were sitting directly at the front, who had actually got a good view of what was happening and realised the danger we were in.

Lisa: And did they do anything?

Katharine: No. They were just sat there. Just panicking. Well, you would, wouldn't you?

The first thing was getting an ambulance for the driver. We've got a coach mobile telephone, so I managed to call my depot, and they immediately alerted the emergency services. An ambulance arrived pretty quickly, in about ten minutes, and took the driver away. And as soon as the ambulance came the police came alongside with them. And the police were great. But then we were all left, stuck on the motorway, waiting for another driver to come and take us on to London.

Lisa: So in those ten minutes before the ambulance and police arrived, what did you do?

Katharine: In those ten minutes?

Lisa: Yes. When you had stopped the coach, and before the ambulance and police arrived, did you turn and look at everybody and what did you say to them?

Katharine: I think I was actually in shock by then. I knew that I had to control the whole situation because I was basically – well, not in charge, but people on the bus were looking to me to take control. Luckily there was a nurse on board. She and her husband were to fly to Vancouver from Heathrow, and she attended to the driver.

The others were just stunned more than anything. Nobody was hurt. I told everyone what had happened, and what was going to happen, and they were fine.

I think I was just running on adrenaline, because I managed to hold Air Canada for twenty minutes for the nurse and her husband to catch their flight. And I was making all sorts of phone calls for other people. There were triplets at the back of the coach – I think they must have been about my brothers' age at the time, fourteen or fifteen – and I was keeping an eye on them. And just generally keeping everybody calm.

Lisa: Were you calm yourself inside?

Katharine: Not at all! Not at all! No, I was just running on adrenaline. It had all happened so quickly. I think the worst time was after the danger was over. I didn't feel anything at the actual moment, until after it. I mean, for days after it.

And then of course the police turned up with the ambulance, and the police . . . do you know, it's really fuzzy, Lisa, I can't really remember much after the police arrived.

Lisa: Why is it that you can't remember?

Katharine: So much attention has been brought to what actually happened – but I can't remember. It was all of a fuzz. All I do remember is that about half an hour afterwards a relief driver came. The police stayed with me until then. The relief driver took over the coach and then we just ran straight into London like a normal service.

Lisa: And then that was it – you took all the people straight to London? You just carried on doing your normal job?

Katharine: Yeah. And on the way back too. I was doing all the usual things, making drinks, serving teas and coffees.

Lisa: Really? And were people talking about what had happened?

Katharine: On the way back nobody knew anything about it, and I wasn't going to tell them. I just wanted to get home, to tell you the truth. I was shaking. My car was parked at the depot, where I should have finished my shift. I had this nail appointment to go to. It is what I was thinking about. And because it was so late . . .

Lisa: *What time did the accident actually happen?*

Katharine: I think it must have been at eleven o'clock, quarter past eleven-ish.

Lisa: *So what time were you due back from London?*

Katharine: About . . . one thirty? And my nail appointment was for four o'clock. So I could have just made it. And this was quite funny. Because I was so late, I asked my mum to pick me up from Bournemouth Station, because the appointment was in Bournemouth and . . .

Lisa: *Did she know what had happened?*

Katharine: Well, I had phoned her up. I said, 'You'll never believe what happened . . . blah blah blah . . . Anyway, pick me up, because I've got this nail appointment.'
So I went for the nail appointment.
And then an hour, an hour and a half later, I turned up to pick my car up from the depot – and it was bedlam, because the press were all there. And my manager was going mad, saying, 'Where have you been?'
I said, 'Nowhere. I've been having my nails done.'

Lisa: *And your mum literally whipped you straight off for your nail appointment – and none of the press were there then?*

Katharine: Not at my nail appointment! No!

Lisa: *So what were you thinking while you were having your nails done? Were you talking about it with your mum?*

Katharine: Yeah. She couldn't believe it. I said, 'Mum, you wouldn't believe what's just happened.' But the way

I was looking at it, you've just got to sort of get on with it.

Lisa: And how did your mum react? Was she like 'Oh! Oh!'?

Katharine: Yeah. She was.

Lisa: Was she really worried?

Katharine: I think it was more, 'Thank God.' She was more happy and relieved that it had all ended happily and I was safe.

Lisa: And when you sat down to have your nails done, did you talk about it then, to the woman? What did she say?

Katharine: Yeah. She said, 'Well done.'
   And I felt quite proud. But later on, when all the press were involved – you know, calling me a heroine and things – you think, 'Hang on! I haven't done anything all that special. I've just done something in a split second . . . what my head told me to do . . .'

Lisa: Yeah, but if you hadn't run to the front of the coach and taken the wheel, then all those forty-odd passengers . . . could be . . .

Katharine: Yeah. God knows . . .

Lisa: Do you see yourself as a heroine?

Katharine: No. Not at all. I mean, everyone I've spoken to afterwards was saying, 'Well done. It's excellent.' I don't know. It's bizarre. I'm glad it happened, obviously – I mean I'm glad that I reacted the way that I did react, but I don't think it was exceptionally brave.

I can't understand anybody looking at it as something amazing. It's just something that happened in a couple of seconds. The same way as if you drop a ball and it rolls into the road, you quickly run after it and pick it up – you know that sort of way.

Lisa: Like instinctively?

Katharine: Yes. That's right.

Lisa: But you were at the back of the coach, so somebody at the front of the coach – their instinct wasn't the same. Their instinct wasn't to quickly grab the wheel of the coach and start to steer it to safety . . . so there must be something in you. All the different people whom I've met who have all done different amazing things. I always wonder what made them do it. Was it instinct? Unless it happens to you, you don't really understand.

Anyway, let's get back to the nail appointment!

Katharine: (*Laughs*) I don't want to talk about it any more!

Lisa: OK. Well who was the first person to say to you, 'Well done'? Was it the people on the coach?

Katharine: I don't actually think they did.

Lisa: (Laughs) You had just saved all their lives and nobody says, 'Thank you'?

Katharine: (*Laughs*) Just 'What time do we get to Victoria?' Oh, no. Probably they must have done. It's only I can't really remember. It's like a real fuzz. I'm sure they must have done. Yeah.

Lisa: *What about the coach driver? What happened to him?*

Katharine: He didn't die or anything. I heard he was all right. And I was thankful. I didn't really know him that well, so I wasn't expecting him to phone up and say anything. He didn't ever go back to work again. I'm sure that in his heart of hearts he's grateful and happy about the way it all ended, but at the end of the day he probably felt a bit stupid as well. Maybe he shouldn't have gone back to work so soon after his major heart surgery.

Lisa: *OK. And did the police and ambulance men say anything to you?*

Katharine: The police said, 'Well done. You've done a good job.' And they actually put me down for an award for bravery.

Lisa: *What about the people on the coach? Did you ever hear from any of them afterwards? Did any of them write to the depot or anything?*

Katharine: Yeah, they did. I got a couple of nice letters from people – and here's me saying they didn't thank me. I got a couple of nice letters congratulating me and telling me how well I'd done. And I think it was one of the passengers who nominated me for the People of the Year Award, which I felt very proud of. It's nice to know that you've touched somebody's life in a way that they remember you and think of you.

Lisa: *Good. So then you got back from this nail appointment to your depot . . . your mum dropped you off. And when you got there, what was happening?*

Katharine: Oh! It's mayhem! There's everyone there: all these photographers and television cameras – Meridian Television were there – and my manager is flapping around telling me what to say and what not to say and I'm thinking, 'I'm not having any of it. What's it got to do with you? You weren't there!'

But I tell you what. It was then that it hit me. It was like, 'Wow! I've done something really special!'

You know, because it's not an everyday thing to finish work and find there are all these photographers and press waiting, just wanting to talk to you.

Lisa: *What sort of things were the reporters asking you? For the local papers you must have been 'local heroine'. All that sort of thing?*

Katharine: Basically very much the same as you are asking me now: what had happened, how had I reacted, what made me react like that? It seemed like loads of them, and there were all these cameras going off, and they were all going, 'Katharine! Katharine! Katharine! Der? Der? Der?'

And I was trying to answer all of them. You know what it's like, when you're not used to it? You can't really ignore anyone. And there's my manager telling me what to say.

Lisa: *I should think, you being twenty-one and really, really pretty and with your jolly personality as well, they thought it was their birthday. I know from my own experience that they think, 'Ooh, good, someone young who will chat away!' They love it, and especially when you're a heroine as well, the heroine of the day.*

So at that point, when you were talking to them, did you think then, 'I've done something really special?'

Katharine: Yeah. I did. I mean, that's when it really did sink in. It was just *so* bizarre. I thought, 'Are all these people really here for me?'

It was because of people telling me that what I'd done was so good that made me think of it like that. Do you see what I mean? I mean, if there hadn't been so much press attention, it probably wouldn't have hit me in the way that it did.

Lisa: And how did you feel when it did hit you?

Katharine: I was happy and proud. Proud because people said that I'd saved forty-six lives . . .

Lisa: Were you stressed out that they were asking you all those questions, or were you quite calm?

Katharine: I was *hungry!* It had been such a long day!

At the end of the day, I'm just a normal girl – you know, go to work, do my job, go home, have my dinner, go out with my friends. And it had been such a long day and I hadn't eaten a thing, and it was going on and on, and they wanted all these photographs . . . And it didn't seem real . . . it felt fake to me, because I'm not used to that kind of attention.

Lisa: It is scary, isn't it? One day you're just an ordinary person living a normal life, and then suddenly you are flung into the limelight. So what did you do when it was all over? After they had all thanked you – did you just go home?

Katharine: Yes. I just went home and sat at table and had tea with my mum.

I really didn't have too much time to think about it all that night, because I was trying to focus on my Virgin interview the next day, and that was all I really wanted to do. It was all I had been thinking about for weeks beforehand, concentrating on it. I couldn't sleep a wink because of what had happened. I had to get up the next day – I was working in the morning – and then I had to go for the interview in the afternoon.

Lisa: You just went for your normal job in the morning? Did you ever think, 'Oh my gosh, this might happen again?' Did you have any bad reaction to it all?

Katharine: No, none at all. I was just running on adrenaline. Except that I hadn't slept a wink. That night I couldn't sleep. I just could not.

I got up early because I was starting at some silly time, like five o'clock in the morning. We drove the coach from the depot to Poole and when we stopped outside a newsagent I went in and brought some newspapers, and I was on the front page of every paper. There was a big spread in the *Daily Mail*. And I thought, 'This is just crazy!'

Lisa: And how did you feel then, when you saw yourself on the front page?

Katharine: I felt really, *really* happy. They jazz it up, don't they? It's like a couple of seconds of something, and all of a sudden it's a really big thing. Column inches about it all. I've kept all the cuttings, but I can't remember what they say.

I think I took it quite well. I thought, 'This is great. This is great.' Well, it's not every day that you see yourself in the headlines, is it? And I did laugh. I thought it was funny.

Lisa: Right. So you've got all the newspapers and you've looked at them and the coach driver's looked at them. Did the passengers on the coach realise who you were?

Katharine: The next morning? I don't think so. I couldn't say anything myself. I was quite shy about it. But when we got to Victoria Station the staff were looking at me, and the other coach stewardesses were looking at me, and my colleagues at Victoria Coach Station were congratulating me and saying, 'Well done, well done.' And I suppose I was lapping it up a bit!

And when we were coming back from London when I was finishing my shift there were a couple of people on the coach who recognised me, and I loved it. I really loved that, because they recognised me. And I think you enjoy it more because it's not an everyday occurrence.

Then my mum drove me into Crawley, because we have some friends who live there, and my interview with Virgin Atlantic was at Gatwick. We got to my mum's friend's house, where of course I got some more attention.

Meantime I had my interview, an interview I'd been concentrating on for weeks prior to the incident. I'd done really well. I was the only one out of thirty girls to get through to the interview stage.

And the sad part is, I just totally lost it. I was shaking like anything – I couldn't even think of my own name. I was so, so tired. I was exhausted by the previous twenty-four hours. It had been a complete out-of-this-world experience. And then I had to do a maths exam. I was looking and looking at the questions, and I had about ten minutes to do them all, and I just couldn't think straight to work the sums out.

I didn't get the job.

I was . . . upset, because I had really prepared for it and I really wanted it.

Lisa: Do you think it was because of what happened the day before? Did it affect you?

Katharine: It did affect me. I wouldn't change it for the world, but it definitely affected the way I was concentrating . . . I mean, I couldn't concentrate. Not at all. It kept coming back to me.

And it was all the hype and the publicity. I got carried away with it, to tell you the truth. Seeing myself in the papers and on television. I think, the actual thing itself, the way I look at it, it was like a split-second decision – and it was over. And I think the worst thing you could do is to keep on thinking about what could have happened. I try not to think about what could have happened. It didn't. That's good enough for me.

Lisa: So after the interview, you went back home feeling pretty sad, then?

Katharine: Yeah. Sad. And pretty let down. I thought they might have given me a bit of leeway because of what had happened. But fair enough, they've got their guidelines and they've got to stick to them.

When we got home the coach story was on the local television news, which my auntie taped for me. And for up to a week later there were snippets about it in the papers. Just what I'd been up to, and what happened to the driver.

Lisa: They didn't pry into your private life?

Katharine: (*Laughs*) No! No! Got a lucky escape with that one! There's no need for it, is there? At all.

Lisa: What about your friends? And your boyfriend? How did they react?

Katharine: They were like, 'Wow!' And I enjoyed it, but I was embarrassed by it all as well. They kept going on about it – they still do go on about it. I'm like, 'All right! All right!' (*Laughs*) I mean it's been three, *over* three years now. But people still do say, 'I remember you . . . blah, blah, blah.'

I mean I'm proud. I *am* proud. I still get embarrassed though, when people mention it.

Lisa: So when you were invited to the Hilton Hotel in London, and you were going to get the People of the Year 1996 Award – how did you feel?

Katharine: I was honoured. Absolutely honoured. It was nice to know that I'd done something that affected somebody's life and for them to recommend me for such an award.

Lisa: And your brothers came with you. How did they feel about you?

Katharine: They must have been thirteen coming up to fourteen at the time, and they were so proud of their big sister! It was such a big day, with celebrities, and trumpets playing. It was unreal.

Lisa: But it was nice?

Katharine: Oh yes, it was nice.

Lisa: Were you nervous when you had to go on stage? Because I kept thinking I was going to fall over!

Katharine: I normally have so much to say, but just as my name was called out to go up, my mind went blank, and I thought, 'Oh God, please, please don't let me make a fool of myself up there.' And I was fine. I enjoyed it. Everybody enjoyed it.

Lisa: What have you done with the glass bowl thing they give you? Mine's in my mum's house.

Katharine: It's still in the box. I should get it out really, shouldn't I? Bit late now.

Lisa: Put it up. What else did you get? The police gave you something? Did National Express give you a reward?

Katharine: I got a certificate from the police. They said I'd averted what could have been a major accident on the motorway. With it being the first day of the Easter holidays there was a lot of traffic on the road. Anything could have happened. It could have been a multi-vehicle pile-up.

And I got a weekend away in Amsterdam from the National Express! (*Laughs*) They congratulated me and it was nice. It was good. I went away with my mum and my cousin. It was brilliant. Such a laugh.

Lisa: You work for Heathrow Express now — the trains between Paddington and Heathrow. Have you told them about it?

Katharine: No, never. I never tell anyone. Even on the application forms when they ask you things like, 'Have you done anything out of the ordinary?' I won't use it. I can't use it. I think that, one, they won't believe me, and two, they'll think that I'm bragging. So I don't. If people ask me — which they don't tend to! — if I've ever saved anyone's life . . . (*Laughs*) Well, if it comes up, then I'll mention it.

Lisa: *Would you do it again?*

Katharine: Definitely. I couldn't not. I'm really interfering! I've got to be there! I'm always doing stupid things. I mean, that wasn't stupid at all. But I remember once I witnessed a person across the road from my mum's house, getting burgled. So what did I do? Instead of calling the police I started to chase him. I chased and caught up with this burglar. My mum called the police, but I decided to chase him myself.

I followed him to his house, and I was really mad, because my car had been broken into just a couple of days earlier. So I just turned into a psycho, and he must have thought, 'What the hell's going on here? There's some psycho woman following me asking for the video back!'

(*Laughs*) He gave me the video back! So I took the video back to the neighbours! And that was that!

Lisa: *So today, if a train kind of . . . ?*

Katharine: God, I hope I don't have to do that on a train!

Lisa: *If something happened to the train driver?*

Katharine: I'll have to be there, won't I?

Lisa: *Ah. You're a nice girl, aren't you? Do you have a faith? Do you believe in God?*

Katharine: I do. I'm a Roman Catholic. My family were all born Italian, so not too strict! I believe in God and I have a faith, but I don't go to Mass. I do pray before I go to sleep. I've got two uncles who both died young, and a friend who recently died, and I speak to them . . . Well, I speak to God and tell him to say 'hello' every so often.

Lisa: What about on that day? Did you talk to God then?

Katherine: Do you know, I think God must have been the one person I didn't speak to that day! Sorry, God. But I knew that my time wasn't up.

Lisa: But do you think God was with you that day?

Katharine: Oh, I believe he's always with me. Or somebody – like maybe one of my uncles or my granddad – is around and helping me along.

Lisa: Do you wonder sometimes if the other people on the coach ever think about you?

Katharine: I do actually. I wonder how they felt about it at the time, and if they ever think about it now. It would be nice to know. But I should think they are quite happy that they are still around!

Lisa: Were you sad when it all died down?

Katharine: Not at all. No. I just take life as it comes. I enjoyed it because it wasn't a normal occurrence. I'm not in the papers every day. But I don't think I could handle it all the time.

It is a nice memory. I hate talking like this, I really hate it – but my doing what I did obviously saved people's lives, including my own. And the way I think about it is that if anything had happened to me, my family would have been absolutely devastated, my brothers particularly. We're very, very close. So I'm glad I'm still around for all of them.

The driver recovered. All the other people on the coach were fine. They were glad we were just carrying on. And I was glad just to turn round and get home – to get back for my nail appointment! But can I just say, for the record, that I never *ever* have my nails done normally – it was only for this one interview!

Lisa's Reflections
What Katharine did that day was a quick and instinctive act. To me she is a supreme example of somebody who made all the difference when it really mattered.

If she hadn't had such presence of mind and ability to act quickly and take charge, not only might all the people on the coach have been killed, including Katharine herself, but the coach could easily have slewed across the motorway and collided with drivers coming the other way. There could easily have been pictures of a horrific multiple motorway pile-up on the television news that night. Instead, there were pictures of a pretty, laughing girl; disaster was averted and everyone's life was able to carry on as normal.

I asked Katharine, 'Did she panic?' And she said, 'Not until afterwards.' Not until she turned round to find forty-four pairs of eyes looking at her on the coach! I think in any crisis or moment of danger that's always the case. It's afterwards that the shock sets in.

It's easy to think that it was just a 'near miss', that nobody was hurt, and it wouldn't take much to get over it. But she did suffer from psychological shock. She had come very close to death, and although she doesn't dwell on it, it made her realise how much her family would have suffered if things had turned out differently. I admire the courage and modesty of someone like Katharine, who does the right thing, and then just gets on with their life.

Above all I loved her sense of humour, her personality. I enjoyed the fact that she was so preoccupied about getting back in time for her nail appointment. I can even relate to that. When I was in the ambulance, as the driver was cutting the buttons off my cardigan, and cutting up the sleeve to get it off I said crossly, 'Please don't do that. This cardigan is from Next!'

At the time I was more worried about my expensive cardigan than about my arm. And Katharine was worrying about missing her nail appointment, she had no idea that she was a national heroine with an appointment with the media.

I envied the way she enjoyed every minute of all the attention she got. Everyone involved in the incident was alive and unhurt, so she really could enjoy those awards without any sense of guilt. She had no cause for guilt. She did the right thing, and it all turned out the right way. So she could go on and enjoy being in the limelight, and getting the People of the Year Award.

She had her fifteen minutes of fame – and she was a heroine without sadness. People think it must be a fine thing, being called a heroine. But it isn't always fine. Sometimes there is a long healing process to be gone through before life seems fine again. I only have to think of little Francesca's scarred face to know how much I would give it all up, if I could only put the clock back and change things.

Katharine is the heroine who doesn't need to put the clock back. Nothing bad happened to anybody. She did the right thing, then she had some excitement and fun and attention, and then it was over. She herself sees it as very little, what she did. She doesn't see herself as a heroine.

But she took responsibility, not thinking, 'Who is going to help?' Her attitude was, 'It's got to be me.'

3

Arthur Withey – 'Have-a-go' Pensioner

Building Society Robbery

Bristol, June 1997
Sometimes when people go up to receive their Unsung Heroes Award or the People of the Year Award, the audience are in tears when the award winners talk about what they've done. It wasn't like that with Arthur. Everybody was laughing, not only because there is something kind of funny about a pensioner who used to be an all-in wrestler, but mainly because Arthur's a really feisty character with a great sense of humour. In 1997 Arthur, then aged seventy, tackled and thwarted a would-be bank robber, aged twenty, at his local building society.

When I telephoned him to ask him if he'd be in my book, he said he'd love to and invited me to go down to see him in Bristol. But then he had to go into hospital for an operation, so it was postponed until after the People of the Year Awards for 1999. We were both guests at that event, and Arthur came up to me and said, 'Hello, I'm Arthur. You must be Lisa. I recognised your voice straight away.'

I went to see him a week later at his home in Bristol. There's a wonderful picture of a train painted by Arthur himself on his living-room wall, and the house is full of his paintings, because he's an artist as well as an ex-wrestler. When I got there, I found him writing letters to his friends who he meets up with when he and his great friend and companion Marge go all round the world on his motor-bike. He made me a cup of tea. I was soon going to be off to Chicago for the Millennium celebrations, so he got out all his maps and showed me the best places to see. He was like a lovely granddad, one who you could sit and listen to all day. He is a real salt-of-the-earth sort of man.

This is a lighter story than some of the others you are going to read about, but it is nevertheless a story of great courage about a real hero.

Arthur's Story

Full name, Arthur Geoffrey Withey. I was born in Bristol but all my relatives originally come from the Somerset marshes, where the withey trees grow, that are used to make cane furniture. So I come from a long line of sticks. I've got a motorcycling friend, and he has a business making cane chairs and settees and all the baskets for the balloons – all out of withey sticks.

I'm just coming up for seventy-three. 'Well preserved' say most of my friends. I'm five ten, five ten and a half. I've shrunk a little bit. I used to be five eleven. Medium build. I'm up to thirteen stone now, but when I was amateur wrestling I was lightweight – ten and a half stone.

I grew up in Bristol. I was a chronic asthmatic all through my young life. Very bad. But after five years in the army, I came out a little bit better, health-wise. Then I went to the gymnasium, took up weight-lifting and freestyle wrestling. I played some rugby as well.

It nearly killed me, but over the years I've realised that all this sport and exercise has done me the power of good, as an asthmatic. I've known asthmatics from here to Australia who are still suffering from something, whether it's a nervous complaint or pollen or whatever. But all my activities in sport did me the world of good. I never became a world champion – won a few medals, but never a great champion. But that doesn't matter. It's what you get out of the sport.

We had a club here in Bristol and I started off there and did reasonably well at it. I wrestled in the Albert Hall twice, Harringay Arena twice, and White City once, all in what was known as the National Wrestling Championships – freestyle. Nothing to do with professional wrestling. This is Olympic stuff. Never won a title, but enjoyed great comradeship. That was all through my twenties and thirties.

Then in my early thirties I emigrated to Canada. I started off in Toronto. I went with another chap, an amateur boxer. We'd both come out of the army. While I was in Canada I got involved with the wrestling there, and weight-lifting. Eventually I gave up the wrestling, in my late thirties, because as you get older there are younger chaps coming along who are a darned sight better.

So I stuck with weight-lifting and I moved to Ottawa, the capital of Canada, and stayed there for another three years. While I was there I coached another friend of mine, Alan Salter – he was bantamweight champion of Canada. I said to him, 'If you get through to the Commonwealth Games in Perth, I'm coming with you.' And he did. He won the championship, so I went to Australia as his coach, to the Commonwealth Games in Perth. Not as a competitor, just as a coach.

And in Perth there were six female relations of my mothers, who had never been back to England, so no one in the family had ever seen them. I met up with them, and then I stayed on in Perth for three years. I worked for the government, in printing. Then I moved to Sydney. But Sydney wasn't my sort of place. I got asthma again, very badly, in Sydney. When it changes from the Indian Ocean the weather is very bad for asthmatics and bronchial people. I couldn't put up with losing work through bad health. So after some fifteen years of living abroad, I thought it was time to come back home to see my parents. So I came back to England.

Then my father was taken ill with cancer, so I helped look after him. I took a job with a printing firm locally. I nursed my father for over two years, until he died. From then on I looked after my mother. She lived for another twenty years after that. She lasted until she was ninety-nine and four months. So I spent my time looking after my mother. Then she died.

I was still a printer, and carried on printing. There weren't many jobs about, so I stuck with the job I had, which was well enough paid, until I retired. And then I took early retirement – thank goodness – and more or less tried to live a life of luxury on my pension. I enjoy painting. I took my motorcycle out all over the world. Got a lot out of being a pensioner. Working well and having a good wage, and looking after your money meant it was a good life . . . And then there was this whole business with the building society.

It was one day in June three years ago, 1997. A normal Monday for me. I just went up to the building society to draw out about two hundred pounds. I can't remember now what it was for. Eleven o'clock in the morning. It's just up the road, along the main road. I walked up. If I have to go and draw out money, I usually do that and then do my shopping afterwards. So I crossed the road, and outside on the pavement was this tall chap in a pale blue tracksuit, with his pixie hood up, and he walked passed the building society at least three times. And I thought it was very peculiar. You don't normally see young men wearing pale blue tracksuits. It just stuck out like a sore thumb. Everybody else was just normal, going about doing their shopping, and in the middle of them doing nothing in particular was this big, tall, coloured fellow in a pale blue tracksuit.

Anyway, I went into the building society. I got up to the counter, and behind me all down the wall was a long string of people waiting to be served. There must have been twelve or fifteen people in the queue. The building itself is rather narrow, with the counters at the far end. I went up to a counter and the chappy behind it was just counting out my money when the commotion started.

'Don't anybody move. I've got a gun. Anybody moves, somebody's going to get hurt.'

And the pale blue tracksuit guy jumped straight over the counter, and started ransacking the drawers and shoving money into his tracksuit top. He'd gone right through all our money at the till I'd been at, and gone into the next one, screaming all the time, 'Don't anybody move. I've got a gun.'

And nobody did move.

I thought to myself, 'This is ridiculous.' In fact I thought at first it was something to do with rag week. University rag week. I just stood there transfixed like the rest of them. Then I realised that this was for real. I thought, 'Nobody's doing anything. This man's going to get away with all our money.' He was really stuffing himself with all this money. He emptied all the tills.

The cashiers just sat back and watched him. They are supposed not to do anything. This is their instruction, apparently. He'd gone to the third teller, still yelling and screaming, 'I've got a gun! I've got a gun. I'll shoot anyone who attempts to stop me.'

But I thought, 'How can he have a gun and use it with his hands full of money at the same time? This is ridiculous. I'm going to do something about this.' So I crouched down behind the counter and I said 'Shhh' to the man next to me. Because I could see he was going to have to come back over the counter in exactly the same place where he had gone over it. There was no other place he could do it, and there was no way out of the back of the building.

All this business was more or less over within two or three minutes. I squatted down behind the counter so he couldn't see me. Then he had to come back over the counter in the same place, as I'd predicted. As he jumped back up to get over the way he came in, I jumped up, grabbed him by the legs and crashed him to the ground. As he hit the deck, the money went everywhere, and a little girl sitting in a pushchair on the side got covered in notes. So she was rich for a short while.

He tried to get away. I got on top of his back and wrestled him as much as I possibly could. There are three steps down. We went head first down these steps, and his trainers came off, and all the money came out of his jacket. Thousands of pounds flying all over the place.

And I'm trying to put a hold on him. But I hadn't been wrestling for thirty years and the difference between him and me was fifty years. This man is twenty years old, much more full of adrenaline than me, and he's trying madly to get to the door. I managed more or less to get a half nelson on him, which is one arm round the back of the neck. We got to the door, me on his back. A couple of others were trying to help by then. In fact one man hurt his wrist trying to help. But everybody else just stood back. If we had all jumped on him and sat on him it would have been easy – but they were all too stunned or something. It was ridiculous. Apart from my money, which it had taken me years to save and put in there, he was pinching all their money as well, and nobody was doing a thing about it.

Lisa: Did you think your life was in danger at any point?

Arthur: No, I never thought along those lines at all.

Lisa: I know he said he'd got a gun but because he had money in his hands you thought he couldn't use it, but he also had some stuffed in his top, and he could easily have had a gun.

Arthur: Yes, but when he jumped back over the counter, he had his hands full, and all your money is done up in rubber bands, isn't it? Well, he had two handfuls of rubber-banded money. Apart from what he had stuffed in his top.

Lisa: But there were other people there, younger people. What made you – aged seventy – think 'I'm going to go for this'?

Arthur: Well, what got me going was thinking, 'My God, it's taken me years to put this money in here. It's all my pension money. And here's a young fellow, getting it all for nothing. And all these people in here, it's their money as well, and they are doing nothing about it.'

It takes a long time to put this money in there, to build up, to give yourself a better life as you get older. And this fellow was grabbing it all for nothing. I wasn't prepared to let him.

So, as I said, I managed to get a half nelson on him just as we got to the door. Now the door was about an inch thick of heavy glass. A heavy door. And somebody must have pushed the door open just as we got there. It hit me on the head, because I was on top of him. I saw stars, and relaxed my hold. In an instant he managed to get to his feet and run outside the door. But the teller who had been dealing with me at the counter, had run through behind us and he managed to catch him and bring him down just outside the door.

The teller and I both got hold of him again outside the door, and the police turned up at exactly that moment, because by then somebody had pressed an alarm button. So the police arrested him just as we all got outside.

Lisa: Were you all right? Were you hurt?

Arthur: Had a couple of bruises on the leg, outside of that I didn't have any injuries at all.

Lisa: And what happened to you then?

Arthur: I sat down on a seat inside. Huffing and puffing, I have to admit. I was really puffing. And one of the women in the place came through and said, 'Mr Withey, have a cup of tea.'

I said, 'Oh yes. That would do me the world of good.'

She gave me the cup of tea and some people there said, 'Gosh! You didn't half give him a going over. It was just like watching the wrestlers you used to see on TV.'

And I said – I didn't remember saying it, but it was quoted back to me later – 'Huh! I might have been a wrestler years ago, but what the hell am I doing it for at my age?'

I had two cups of tea. Made a statement to the police upstairs, at the back of the building. Did my bit of shopping at the supermarket, got some stuff, and then I went home.

When I got in I made myself a nice cup of coffee – in fact I put two slugs of whiskey in it. I thought, 'Gosh! Struth! Boy, am I aching!'

I live on my own, so I didn't tell anybody. I just sat and thought, 'What did I do that for?' You know. And then I fell asleep in the chair.

I have to admit, after all that exertion, I could not put on a T-shirt the next morning. I couldn't even put my trousers on. I was stiff from my ears to my ankles. So all this business that you see on television programmes, when they are fighting like mad, and then you see them over in the bar having a drink, it's a load of rubbish. You stretch your muscles to the point where they are so stiff you can hardly move.

Lisa: Were you brought up to react like that?

Arthur: No, no. It's not in my character to fight. My character's not like that at all. If there's a rumpus in a pub, I'm more likely to pick up my pint and walk out through the door the other end, out of the way. But if I'm in striking distance of someone in trouble, I'd always go for it.

A similar thing has happened twice before in my life. Years ago, when I was living in Toronto, and my friend and I were in Simpson's store looking for shirts or something, we heard a scream. We looked over to the counters on the other side, and this woman was screaming her head off, and a man was running down the aisle. My friend and I ran down the other aisle, and rugby-tackled him. I went for his legs and my friend went for his shoulders, and we ploughed this man into the floor. The floor detective came along, and then the police and they took him away. We saw in the papers later on that he'd thrown carbolic acid in the woman's face, trying to rob her.

The other time was in London, after I'd been to a concert with my cousin. He's a classical clarinettist. We were just returning to his home in Bayswater, and when we got outside his house we heard a scream. There was a fight going on at the pub at the end of his street. Then this man came running up the road. I got behind a car, and as he reached the back of the car I stepped out at the front and – I'm not a boxer, but I landed him one absolute haymaker right in the middle of his face. It split his nose. He went down and smashed a beer mug when he hit the pavement. People had heard all the commotion and reported it, and two cars – two police cars – came into the road, one at the top and one at the bottom, and picked the man up, and that was that.

Lisa: And both of those instances were purely instinctive? You never thought of your own safety?

Arthur: Oh, the first time I was a young man. The second time I was in my late forties. But I don't think it's anything heroic at all. That's not the issue. I happened to be there, and I had to do something.

Lisa: So this time, what happened after that? You fell asleep in your chair – then what happened?

Arthur: The police turned up two days later and asked if I'd had any injuries. I said, 'Well, I've got some scratches on my leg, and I've got a few bruises.'

Then I had to go down to the police station to be photographed, so they could be used as evidence in the court case, when the man went up in front of the judge. I couldn't drive my car, I was still so stiff, but the policeman said, 'Not to worry' and they took me down in the police car, and they brought me back again. And when I got back from the station, there was a reporter at the front door.

That thing I had said, 'I may have been a wrestler once, but what the hell am I doing it for at my age?' Well, someone had picked that up, and somehow someone on the newspapers must have heard.

Then three or four reporters came round. Two from local papers and then after that we had the *Daily Telegraph* and *The Times* here. And then television turned up and all that sort of business. Well, you know all about that, don't you?

Lisa: *What did you think when all these journalists came?*

Arthur: I just thought I hadn't done anything fantastic. Didn't know what all the fuss was about. There was a little strip at the top of the *Sun*, that some of my motor-cycle chums saw, and they had a good laugh. They said, 'Hey! Seventy-Year-Old Big Daddy Flattens Burglar!' Well I never was a fat Big Daddy type at all. It was ridiculous.

Lisa: *Did you buy all the papers the next day to see what they said?*

Arthur: No, well, I got one or two. But it was more other people telling me, 'Oh, I saw your photograph in the *Mail*. Saw your photograph in the *Western Daily Press*.'

I had several phone calls. A friend of mine in Penzance called and said, 'Hey, what have you been doing? I opened my *Telegraph* this morning, and there was your big mug looking at me!' A half page of the *Telegraph* – I have got a copy of that one. And then my cousin in Bayswater, he phones up and says, 'Goodness, gracious me, what have you been up to? I've opened my *Times* this morning, and there you are, in *The Times*.'

Lisa: What did you think?

Arthur: Well, actually, the photograph wasn't too bad. Better than my usual photograph. I'm not one for publicity. I'd rather keep out of it. Bit of fame – it's all over now, anyway. A week later I go up the road to the little bakery there, to buy some pasties, and two ladies said, 'Hello! Hello! We saw you in the papers!'

Lisa: Were you embarrassed?

Arthur: Well, other people were looking, as much as to say 'What's that idiot done?'

Then I pulled into the petrol station and went to pay, and the woman who sits there said, 'I saw your photograph in the paper. Very good photograph, wasn't it?' And I said, 'Which one was this?'

She said, 'The *Western Daily Press*.'

It went on for a couple of weeks like that, people saying they'd seen me.

Lisa: So that went on for a couple of weeks, people stopping you in the street. And what happened then? Because I see you got some awards . . .

Arthur: Yes. I had a phone call – no, a letter from the police. There's a brand-new police headquarters at Portishead and they said I was to go down and receive a Waley Cohen Award. That apparently was something started years ago by a man named Waley Cohen – he was a rich man – for people who had done something or other to help keep law and order. And the police dropped this line to me to go and receive this award. I had to be at Portishead on Wednesday 13 May 1998 to collect this from the Sheriff and all that sort of thing.

Lisa: Did you think, 'Oh, my goodness!'?

Arthur: 'Oh, my goodness', is about right. I didn't think I'd done anything exceptional, you know.

It was a good event. The Sheriff was all done out in his paraphernalia of white stockings and ruffles and a sword. And there was the Chief Commissioner of Police and people like that. There were quite a few other people collecting this award. It's a certificate. Years ago it was a money award, but now it's a certificate. And there were a lot of people, including two young boys who found a man robbing a place, and they got an award for this as well. We got talking over tea and biscuits afterwards.

There was the Sheriff, and the Commissioner of Police, and two inspectors I was talking to, and it turned out they were all motor-cyclists. So the robbery incident was forgotten about while we were all talking motor-bikes. The Sheriff's wife had been talking to Marge – that's my partner, she comes everywhere with me. Then the Sheriff's wife comes over to us and says, 'George, guess what, Arthur and Marge have just been to South Africa!'

'Oh,' he said. 'How nice.'

'Yes. But they've done it on a motor-bike!'

Which we had. We'd just done a month touring South Africa on a motor-bike. So then we were all talking motor-bikes, to hell with the robbery!

Lisa: So you had the certificate . . . and I see that's it in the hall. Don't you feel quite proud of yourself when you see it?

Arthur: Well, it's nice to be recognised when you try to do something.

Lisa: Did the building society recognise it in any way?

Arthur: No. Well, I was given two cups of tea and then a bowl of fruit. Lots of my friends said, 'You should get a money award.' Years ago there used to be a sign up saying that anyone giving information towards the apprehension of a criminal would get a reward. But they've scrubbed that. Anyway, my building society is mean as hell. So there was a letter in the newspaper. Some friends launched an attack on the building society, saying they were stingy for thanking Mr Withey for his help with just two cups of tea and a bowl of fruit. They said a cash reward would have been more appropriate. I didn't know this was going to go in the paper. Then there was the reply: 'A spokesman for the building society says that they did not want to encourage customers or staff to risk their lives by handing out cash rewards for stepping in to try and thwart raiders.'

There. I mean, they're insured against losing money, aren't they? So they couldn't care less if the man gets away with ten thousand pounds. They are covered for that. So the fact that I'm trying to save not only my own money, but everyone else's money, doesn't come into it. It's only worth a bowl of fruit.

And that was it. It was all over. The reporters disappeared. The telephone didn't ring, and I thought 'Thank God that's over.' And it was all over, until . . .

Lisa: Until? Go on . . .

Arthur: Until I got a letter from RADAR in the August – over a year later. August 1998. I thought, 'Crumbs. What's RADAR?' Now I know – the Royal Association for Disability and Rehabilitation. I had to tell them if I would accept it. I telephoned Sheila Graham and said, 'Yes. I'll accept it. Thank you very much.' And she telephoned back, and arranged everything, sent us tickets and an itinerary. I didn't know what sort of occasion it would be.

I couldn't figure out how these people had sorted me out. Apparently they do it by a big committee. They sit down and go through all incidents reported in the press throughout the year and they come to a conclusion as to who is going to receive the award.

Lisa: That's right, yes. And there's only about ten people recognised each year out of the whole of the country.

Arthur: But I didn't expect anything like that at all. Yours was a far more horrific incident than mine. For me, in my case, I think it boils down to this, I'm seventy years of age, I'm tackling a twenty-year-old who is robbing a bank. What a stupid thing to do! And I make a quotation like, 'What the hell am I doing this for at my age?' And I think it was my quotation and the age group that put me into this category.

Lisa: I think you're extremely brave. He said he had a gun. You tackled him. That is bravery. That's not what the normal person in the street would do. But when it's you, you don't see yourself as brave, do you?

Arthur: Yes, I think you've got it right there.

Lisa: So going for the award that November, at the Hilton – you went to the reception the night before?

Arthur: Yes, so I accepted it and made plans. It was good. Marge came with me. I phoned her up and said, 'Guess what? We're going to London to the Hilton.'
She said, 'What's this for?'
I said, 'I've been given another award.'
I told Marg she'd have to buy a new dress and have her hair done. It's quite a do, to walk in and everyone applauds.

We went to 10 Downing Street. We had to be up by eight o'clock. We went in three brand-new taxis. It was interesting, to see all over Number Ten. We looked in the Cabinet office as well.

Lisa: Did you meet Dave Hurst, who's also in my book?

Arthur: Yes, yes. That was marvellous, what he did. He's blind, and goes into the sea to pull someone out. I've got his address, and said we'll look him up one day.

I didn't want to say anything when I was up on the stage, but I was picked out, when Sue MacGregor came forward and asked me a few questions about what I had done. Then she said, 'Will you be doing anything like this again?'

I said, 'No, I'm not going to make a habit of clobbering bank robbers. I'd rather be riding my motorbike.'

Everyone laughed and she said, 'Where do you go?'

I said, 'We've just come back from South Africa.'

She said, 'What? On the motor-bike?'

I said, 'Yes.'

She said, 'On your own?'

I said, 'No, my partner Marge is sitting down there, she was perched on the back.'

'Good heavens!' she said.

There was a little bit on the midday news in London. The local newspapers didn't pick it up. I don't know if it was in the London newspapers, because I didn't buy one. There's been nothing much since then. But now there's your book.

Lisa: I wanted to ask you if you had a faith?

Arthur: I'm not terribly religious – well, not religious at all. Church of England, basically, but . . . faith . . .

Lisa: I've got a very strong faith. I believe God helped me that day, and every day since, really.

Arthur: But it's faith in your inner self, really, isn't it? It's your determination to get through. You've got to pull through. You've got to have faith in yourself, whether it's in God or not. Some don't. I don't think it even enters their thinking. They just think, 'Poor me. I'm ill.' But I don't think you need to be highly religious to have faith in yourself.

Lisa: Yes. I could easily have thought I didn't want to leave the house again. But I thought, no, why should I let one man wreck my life? So I just got up and got on with life. There's so much more to look forward to, and that's behind me now.

Do you ever think about what happened to you now? Do you ever have nightmares about it?

Arthur: No. I go to bed to sleep. I'm a gonner.

I still deal with the same building society, but nobody knows me there now. With these businesses, nobody knows you anymore. They change the personnel so often, that you are not a part of the society anymore. You are just a number.

I continued to pop in, and for a while there were two people there who remembered me – the teller who I'd been dealing with, and one of the women. They knew me by name. Whenever I went in they always said, 'Good morning, Mr Withey.'

I have sometimes stood there, waiting to be served, and thought, 'By God, he didn't half leap over that counter.' I have stood there and visualised what happened, and all the money on the floor.

Lisa: Would you do it again?

Arthur: Like I said before, if I were in striking distance, like at a handbag snatch or something, I would do something. It's not in my nature to stand by and say, 'Oh dear, oh dear.' But it would have to be right in front of me. I couldn't run. Those days are gone.

I've always been a loner. I've always lived alone. All the years in Canada and Australia. Marge would tell you, 'He's his own man.'

I'll tell you one thing, talking about faith. There's a humour that comes out of this, with lots of people. You've got to have some humour, goodness gracious. You can get over a lot of your problems with humour.

I've just had an operation for cancer of the prostate. I beat two women and a little boy to the toilet, pushing my trolley with all the bags hanging off it. I reckon I got up to half a mile an hour down the hospital corridor at one stage.

When I went to the pub after the operation, someone said, 'How are you, Arthur?'

I said, 'Oh, I'm in stitches!'

And we're all laughing our heads off. If you can't laugh at all these minor tragedies in life, you're a dead duck.

Lisa's Reflections

When Arthur told me the story he was doing all the actions – and he made it sound really funny. Crouching behind the counter, all the money fluttering down on the little girl in the pram, himself huffing and puffing when it was all over. When he told me he had been a wrestler, that made me laugh even more. I think that was what made everyone laugh at the People of the Year Awards, because he was this feisty old-age pensioner who rides around the world on a motor-bike, and who used to be an all-in wrestler. Arthur tells his tale almost like a story from the old Wild West – who was going to be quickest on the draw?

I think that maybe what Arthur represents are the values of the older person. He thought about his own money that he'd worked so hard for all those years. He thought it was his pension money that he goes on his holidays with. He couldn't understand why nobody else seemed bothered. The irony was, he needn't have bothered either. They are all insured against that sort of thing these days. But that wouldn't have been Arthur's way. He thought about what was real to him.

He behaved like an old-fashioned gentleman – he wouldn't let the young thug get away with it, but for reasons that wouldn't mean anything to most people any more. The consequences could have been dreadful – if the man had turned his gun on Arthur. He took a big risk. But he didn't see it like that. He just thought he was doing what was right in his own book. Arthur didn't mention this, but although this guy didn't in fact have a gun, it said in the paper afterwards that he did have a knife. It got knocked off him when Arthur tackled him.

I don't know if I'd be able to think that quickly – to be able to realise that even if he had a gun, he couldn't use it because his hands were full of money. I don't think many people would have thought like that.

Arthur was fit, but he wasn't a big man. Not at all. But by his action, he bought time for everyone else to wake up and come and help to overpower the man – although even then not everybody did. And what is so strange is how Arthur said that a similar thing had happened twice before in his life. That was also true of the first two heroes, Dave and Katharine. It makes me wonder if it is a certain type of person who reacts like this.

One thing that Arthur said made me think about my

own situation. He said, 'The police came just in time.' But they didn't for me. In my case, the police didn't come until it was all over. Then they were running around like mad trying to find this man, and I was just standing there. I remember this so well, because I often had nightmares about it afterwards. I was standing in a classroom with all glass windows, with one of the nursery nurses putting towels round my arms to staunch the blood, and one of the mums came running in shouting, 'He's got a gun! He's got a gun!' and I remember thinking, 'I've been through all of this – and now he's going to shoot me.'

Arthur got quite a bit of publicity, but he didn't want to go in for it. I asked him if he got embarrassed when people recognised him in the street. I asked because I find I never know what to say when it happens to me. It's not like being a celebrity for being a professional model or actress or something. If they say, 'I know your face, but where from?' It's not like I can say, 'Oh, I'm the machete heroine.' So it's embarrassing. You can't say anything.

Arthur is someone who believes in himself. He's got that get-up-and-go – 'I'm not just going to sit here and moan.' That's why at seventy-three he's off round the world on his motor-bike with Marge. How many other seventy-three-year-olds have saved their pension to go on adventures like that? They probably could, but so many people let life grind them down. They sit and moan about how the bus is late, and their packet of cheese isn't big enough. Arthur really lives his life to the full, and I admire that. I like to think that when I'm seventy-three I'll be the same. I hope so.

4

Daniel Gallimore
– Dare to be a Daniel?

Showboat Public House, Horfield

31 May 1996

Daniel is another 'have-a-go' hero and he also comes from
Bristol, like Arthur, but unlike any of the three earlier
stories in this book, Daniel's story does not yet have a
happy ending. It is an example of an act of bravery that
had disastrous consequences for the hero. He saw three
men assaulting someone he knew outside a public house.
He went to intervene, and two of them turned on Daniel,
leaving him with a fractured skull, broken neck and
eventual blindness.

   I went to talk to Daniel and his mum, Sylvia, at their
home near Bristol. We sat in their conservatory and Daniel
told me a bit about himself.

Daniel's Story

My name is Daniel Edward Gallimore. I'm twenty-five, born on 13 September 1974. I now live back with my mam and my dad in Horfield, Bristol. My mum's called Sylvia, my dad's called Richard. I've got two older brothers: Adam, twenty-six and Joe who is twenty-eight.

I'm five foot eleven. Blue eyes. I used to be really skinny but now I'm well built, thanks to the drugs they have put me on. I used to have really white-blonde hair when I was little, but now it's sort of browny-dark. It's probably got gold bits in at the moment, because if Mum has a little bit of dye left over from doing her own hair, she sticks it on mine. I end up with multicoloured hair.

Ever since I was eight years old I've had this thing called Bechet's disease. It doesn't matter how you pronounce it – we usually call it *Beshay's*. It's a chronically progressive illness. You get ulcers all through your mouth and throat and down your mucus glands. You can get ulcers in your eyes, fatigue and stiff joints. You get horrendous headaches, and it can lead to meningitis, which I've had three times.

They think a trauma triggers it off, because apparently everyone's got it in their bloodstream, but it's only a few people who are unlucky enough to actually get it. When I was eight years old I was playing with a friend in my local park near to our house, and a gang of bigger boys came over and tried to nick our ball – we were playing football – and I wouldn't let them. So they started to beat us up.

I ended up in hospital for a week. Black eye, cuts and bruises, a kick to the ribs that damaged my kidneys. They think the trauma of that is what probably triggered off the Bechet's. I was in hospital again later the same year for about three weeks with ulcers, on an intravenous fluid drip because you can't drink when your mouth fills up with ulcers. It isn't very nice. After that I'd get a really serious attack about once a year, and have to go to hospital. I'd have minor attacks two or three times a year, where I'd just stay in bed at home for a couple of weeks.

I was like all young boys. I wanted to be a footballer, a famous sports star or whatever. But I obviously couldn't do that, because of this illness. I was tired all the time. And I'm slightly dyslexic, so schoolwork was always difficult too. But when you're eight you don't realise the implications. You just live your life as best you can when you are not ill. And I used to enjoy my life. Well, I still do enjoy my life. It's just harder now.

I left Corston Grammar School at eighteen and went straight into a job at ACM – Applied Computer Maintenance. I was on a low, trainee wage, because I was also doing a day-release course for one day a week at college. I was working to get qualifications in computer maintenance, which I passed after two years. But even then ACM weren't prepared to put my wage up, because I had been taking quite a bit of time off work with the Bechet's.

At Corston Grammar School we had had a really nice headmaster who liked me. Mum and Dad both worked at the school, and the headmaster asked me if I wanted a job there looking after the computer networks for the school. So I thought, OK, why not? I had to go round teaching the kids how to use all the software, like Word for Windows, keeping the network running, installing bits of printers and whatnot. It was really, really good. I had great fun for the next six months.

I had got my own one-bedroom flat when I was with ACM. At twenty-one years of age I had a girlfriend, Sarah, my own flat, a car and a job I enjoyed, so life was good.

Then came Friday 31 May 1996. It was school half-term, so I wasn't working. Apart from that I don't really remember much about the early part of the day. In the evening, after spending some time with my brothers and parents at a snooker club that we all belong to, I drove Sarah to our local pub, the Showboat, in Gloucester Road, Horfield. I was playing pool, and not drinking much because I was driving. Sarah had a girlfriend with her.

For some reason I had walked out of the pub at about half nine, quarter to ten-ish, and stood outside talking to various people. We knew everyone there – it was our local. I wandered a little way down the road where you could sit on the railings. I was talking to a lad I knew, and suddenly there was this disturbance going on outside the pub behind us. Sarah was still inside.

It must have been nearly half past ten, I think, when this actually happened. Three men were beating up another man who I knew slightly from the pub. Wayne used to be in the band that played there. I didn't know him well. I just knew him to say 'hi' to. So I watched for a minute or two, as you do . . .

I was sitting there watching these men having a go at him, but then I thought, 'Things aren't quite right here. He looks to be in a bit of pain.' They were actually hitting him quite hard and there was blood.

So I foolishly wandered up to them and said to them, 'Don't you think he's had enough?'

One of them said, 'No, I don't think so.' And hit him again.

I said, 'I really think he has had enough.' And I tried to pick Wayne up off the pavement, to pull him away. That was when they turned and started hitting me, punching me in the face . . .

It's instinctive when you see someone in trouble, to go over and try and do something to help. You just go in. You think you're invincible. And I thought that I had company with me, because there were plenty of other people around. Otherwise I probably wouldn't have gone over on my own. I think Wayne was on his knees by this time, with another man standing over him. He was definitely bleeding.

There were three men, but I think it was only one or two of them who actually hit me, and I fell backwards over the railing. I then very foolishly got up again. I hadn't wanted to stay down on the ground in case one of them came over and started kicking me. So I stood up and one of them punched me again and knocked me out. I fell backwards, hit my head on the kerb, which punctured my skull and broke my neck and led to all the other complications that followed from that. I think Wayne only suffered a black eye and a broken nose.

I don't remember much about the fight – all this is mainly what I've been told. Apparently there were thirty eye-witnesses. It's always bothered me, that. If there were all these witnesses, why did it happen in the first place?

Sylvia (Daniel's Mum):   This is what everybody I've asked has told me. Daniel was sitting outside with this other lad, and all these people walked past while Wayne was being beaten up. Daniel was the only one who went to help him. After Daniel had been knocked out a couple of girls came out to tell these lads what they thought of them – and they got punched. One got thrown across a car and one got kicked in the eye. Then Kate, Joe's girlfriend, got kicked in the face as she was protecting Joe, who was holding Daniel after he fell. And the lad that Daniel had been sitting with – I think he did go down to help Daniel, but he was being lifted off the ground by his throat by one of the lads. But nobody else helped at all. And nobody even sent for the police. And there were at least thirty people there – if they had all converged, nothing would have happened. It wasn't until it was all over that everybody rushed to call an ambulance.

Daniel: I was knocked out, totally out of it. The ambulance came and I regained a bit of consciousness in the ambulance, because the lights weren't flashing and I said something stupid like, 'Oh, I want lights . . . Where are the lights?' I could still see perfectly well at this stage. But I was in and out of consciousness for most of that first week that I was in hospital.

One of the boys at the pub telephoned my mum and said, 'Dan's been hit.' Mum thought he meant hit by a car. So she turned up at the pub just as the ambulance was pulling away. One of the boys there pointed to this pool of blood and said to her, 'That's what happened to Dan.'

The police were called, but they didn't really want to do anything about it because they thought it was just a pub fight on a Friday night, and what do you expect? Just another pub brawl. The men who had done it were seen wandering off up the Gloucester Road afterwards.

I had a fractured skull from ear to ear, right to the corner of my eye. And I had a hairline fracture to my neck. My face was all swollen and bruised where they had punched me. They were the main injuries to start with.

I was in a normal ward for a week. There was a mix-up with the X-rays and the hospital thought I was just a bit beaten up. Then on the Saturday morning I had a fit – and went into a coma. My mum came in quite early that morning to see me. She was walking down the corridor when these nurses rushed past her into my ward. And as she wandered in, she saw me being revived by all these doctors. They told her she'd have to leave. She said, 'Don't be silly, that's my son.'

Sylvia: That Saturday morning I thought I'd go in early to see him, then go to the market, and then pop back to see him again later. So I got to the hospital at quarter to eight. Walked up the corridor – the crash team were running down the corridor with all the alarms going off. I literally arrived at that moment. I followed them in and Daniel had had a fit and arrested in the bed. I just stood there. I watched them, almost like it wasn't real, like an episode of *Casualty*. They were shouting all the time and doing the shock treatment. Then this nurse looked up and said, 'It's all right. He'll be fine.'

I said, 'Don't be ridiculous.' I thought I was standing there watching him die – that's what it looked like to me. It was the ultimate nightmare.

Then a doctor came out and explained that he'd had a minor stroke because his brain had swollen up. He said, 'We don't honestly think he's going to survive. I would suggest that you get your family together.'

I ran and phoned Adam, who is the most sensible. I didn't say too much. I just said he looked pretty bad, because I didn't want him to drive in like a lunatic. Joseph and Adam came and then Joseph went to get his father, because I had the car.

Adam and I were standing outside this room where they stabilise you. Then the doctor came out and said, 'I'd like you to come in, but possibly to say goodbye to him. We may not get him as far as the Intensive Care Unit.'

We went in, and he had so many wires coming out of him, he just looked as though he was dead. The brain swells beyond the capacity of the skull and everything closes down. He went into a coma that day, and he was in the ICU for six and a half weeks, and for four and a half weeks of that he was on life-support.

His eyes were wide open the whole time. They had to keep putting jelly on to keep them from drying out. His pupils were huge. They never changed. It didn't look real. I can understand why people do switch off life-support machines. I was convinced that there was nothing going on, that he was brain-dead. We were making bets to try and cheer ourselves up about what he would do first when he did come round. Then one day he moved his foot very slightly. I went absolutely hysterical.

Daniel: I was in a coma, with my eyes and my mouth wide open. As a result of all the tests they did they thought that my eyes were perfectly OK, but that I was probably going to be deaf. As it turned out, when I came round I was blind, but I could hear perfectly well. Now I'm totally blind in my left eye. I can just see a bit of light and dark shapes and shadows and things wandering about with my right eye. But I couldn't tell you what they are.

Coming round from a coma is not at all how they show it in the movies, with the person coming round and saying, 'Hi, Mum!' You have no idea what is going on. It takes months and months – years even – to come completely out of a coma. They say it will probably take me five years to completely wake up. So I've still got another two years to go – which is quite a frightening thought.

Sylvia: When he first came round he was very disturbed, very fidgety. Not speaking sensibly or anything. Eventually they took the trachea tube out, and gave him an oxygen mask. It wasn't until he could start to speak again that we discovered that he couldn't see. That was why he was so frightened-looking all the time. He must have been in hell – but nobody in the hospital even suggested that he might have a problem with his eyes. So then they sent him to the eye hospital, and three months later they sent us a report telling us what we already knew – that he couldn't see.

Daniel: I didn't really twig it at first – that I was blind. I mean, obviously I couldn't see, but it didn't register. I had so many other things going on that I didn't take it in. I was having a lot of treatment and physiotherapy. Even when you are still in a coma the nurses come around and stretch your legs and try to get the blood flowing round your body. Afterwards you have to carry on with that because you forget how to walk. When I eventually came out of hospital I couldn't walk properly. I had to have a wheelchair for the next year.

I think my emotions about it all are probably switched off even now. I've tried to think about it but whenever I do my mind wanders off onto something else. I don't know why. I just can't do it. It's very strange. I don't even remember all that much about it. I remember things that happened years before, but not much about that whole actual year, 1996.

It happened at the end of May. I came out of hospital in September. I was an outpatient then for a year, and continued with the physiotherapy. My girlfriend Sarah stuck by me all through the time I was in hospital, but we broke up in the following January. I was living at home with Mum by then, and I was fairly bad-tempered, because you get like that after a head injury. You get very frustrated. I couldn't see. I couldn't walk. I couldn't do any of the things I used to do. I used to get quite angry, which I think was probably the main reason why Sarah and I broke up.

Mum and Dad used to have to bathe me and feed me. I couldn't do anything for myself. You have to relearn everything, even down to brushing your own teeth. Every single thing. People don't realise – but how would you make a cup of tea, if you couldn't see? You have to learn how to do that.

Going blind takes away your whole independence. You have to rely on somebody to help you do every single thing. You have to take somebody with you shopping. Like buying clothes – I have to rely on somebody else's opinion of what to wear and what to buy. Just walking down the street, I have to rely on somebody telling me where to go. I can't just think, 'Oh, I'll go out for a drive today, and end up anywhere.' I have to always think where I want to go before I set out.

I had twenty-one and a half years of perfect vision. My eyesight was brilliant. I know what I've lost. Everything.

Sylvia: He is a brave lad. He's always been a brave lad – nothing to do with what he did really. The thing about what he did is that, physically, it wasn't the sensible thing to do.

Lisa: I think with what happened to me, nobody ever talks about how it affected my mum. She had to deal with everything afterwards. She had to deal with the media. And that's forgotten – even in the sense of counselling, that's very often forgotten, because families are affected. Your family was affected – and you've got two other boys as well.

Sylvia: Yes, we were all affected. We all became rather withdrawn I think. Adam was the worst affected. Joseph had his own sons to worry about, to keep him going, but Joseph and Dan were best friends as well as brothers. And although we've got Dan back, we haven't really got our old Dan back. He's a different person. He's bound to be, because he can't do the same things. Joseph always felt as though he's lost his best friend and got another brother.

Lisa: Do you think it has changed you as a person, Daniel?

Daniel: Well, I'm more reserved. I used to be a real jumpy, lively person, always out and about, never indoors. I liked driving about, finding new places. Now I hardly ever go out. I used to be carefree, I used to do something and worry about the consequences afterwards. Now I do worry about the consequences.

But in myself I'm the same person I always was. I wish that other people would realise that. Because all the friends – or all the people that I thought were my friends before – they've all gone. I've got no friends now.

Lisa: Why have they all gone?

Daniel: I wish I knew. I honestly couldn't tell you. They just all vanished.

Lisa: Is that because they can't deal with the fact that you can't see or . . . ?

Daniel: I suppose it must be.

Lisa: Didn't any of them come to see you in the hospital?

Daniel: A few of them did, yes. But then we moved house, and nobody has ever come here. I can't wander round and see them or go down to the pub and catch up in that way. Perhaps they don't realise that.

Lisa: And what about your brothers?

Daniel: Oh, they've been brilliant. If I didn't have Adam and Joe, I don't know what I'd do, because I'd have nobody.

Lisa: So do you go out much now?

Daniel: Not as much as I should do. I go down to the snooker club still. And occasionally to the pub, if Joe or Adam take me there. Adam lives round the corner, so sometimes I wander round to him or he comes round to see me. Other than that, not a lot. Listen to music. Get bored. I should do more really, but I just don't know what to do. I've got no one to go and see. I think, 'Where can I go when there's nowhere to go?'

Lisa: What did the police do, after your mum went round to see them? Did they get the men who'd done it?

Daniel: One of them never got prosecuted at all. Two of them did go to court. They both said it wasn't them, it was the other guy. So one of them got away with it altogether. The other one got fifteen months for the original assault on the man I went to save, and for kicking and punching the two girls. He got fifteen months, but he only served six or seven. He got nothing for hitting me because the judge ruled that it wouldn't be fair to prosecute just one of them, because it might not have been that one who actually did it. There were two of them and they both looked the same, short hair, goatee beards, same sort of clothes. So it wouldn't be fair to prosecute one, when it might have been the other one.

Lisa: And how does that make you feel, that they got away with it?

Daniel: A bit insignificant really. It's like they could just ruin my life, but nobody wanted to do anything about it.

Lisa: Do you still get angry, Daniel?

Daniel: I do, but only when I'm on my own. I punch the pillow. And just think to myself, 'Why me?' And 'How do I do it?' I've had this Bechet's thing since I was eight years old and now I've got this blindness to worry about as well. I've lost my friends, my girlfriend, my job . . .

Sylvia: I told the police the situation and Phil Rodder, the detective in charge, came across. The police wouldn't have taken any action at all if Daniel hadn't gone into ICU, it would just have been written off as another Friday night incident.

I said I wanted these people prosecuted. I knew who they were, because people had told me at the hospital. Everyone at the pub knew them because they'd all been to school together. But that's where we went wrong. Because we'd all been together in the hospital and everyone had talked about it and said their names. You're bound to, aren't you? But that meant they couldn't be prosecuted for some reason.

Daniel's had a tough life, but never made you feel sorry for him. When he was first told he had Bechet's and they told him that most people with Bechet's usually only lived to about forty he just said to me, 'Oh well, then, we'll probably go about the same time. That won't be so bad.' What can you say about something like that?

Lisa: *Do you believe in God, Daniel?*

Daniel: No. I've met quite a few people who are visually impaired or blind, and they all seem to believe in God. It's very odd. I mean, if there was such a being, why would they be blind? That's always puzzled me, really.

Lisa: *Well, if you don't go to heaven, I don't know who will!*

Daniel: Exactly. I'll be *most* disappointed if I don't go! I'll say, 'Remember me?'

Lisa: *Have you had any counselling?*

Daniel: I tried counselling when I was still at the hospital, but I wasn't really interested.

Lisa: And what about now? I didn't want counselling at first either. It was only a year later – and obviously it would be even longer for you – I started to think, 'Oh, why did this happen? How come my whole life has changed? How come I feel differently about things?'

I used to ask all these questions and never knew the answers. Nobody around me could relate to what had happened . . .

Daniel: Nobody has the first clue what it's like.

Lisa: No. That's it. Nobody has. At all. I could probably relate my life before this happened to yours, because we're the same age, and I could probably relate a few feelings to yours now, in regards to how you feel after being attacked. But I think it stops there. Our journeys go off on different paths. I mean what I saw was innocent children being severed across the face and you just can't . . .

Daniel: Yes, well, yours was different because it was innocent little kids and I would hope that everybody would go in and help kids . . .

Lisa: Yes, but at the end of the day, both you and I were innocent too. What did we do? We just tried to do the right thing.

Daniel: Exactly. We just happened to be there at the right – but wrong – time.

Lisa: Do you ever feel nervous? Because, I mean, I look around to see if there's anyone behind me sometimes, or if there's someone quite close by me I get quite tense and nervous. I live with panic a lot, but at least I can actually see the people around me. Do you ever feel quite panicky?

Daniel: Only about the state of the pavements. If you've ever tried walking along the pavements when you can't see, it's a nightmare. There are all these bumps and lumps everywhere, trees in the road. People leave their dustbins lying halfway in the street. You've got roadworks, kerbs – it's just a total nightmare.

Lisa: Do you see yourself as a hero? That you saved someone's life and all that . . .

Daniel: Not really. My mind doesn't work like that. I'm just a regular sort of person, who helped somebody out.

Lisa: You must have had a massive amount of determination at twenty-one to go out to help somebody.

Daniel: Or I was silly!

Lisa: Do you think you were silly?

Daniel: No, not really.

Lisa: How about your family – are they proud of you?

Daniel: I think they are proud, yes. I think so.

Lisa: What do you think will happen to you in the future?

Daniel: I don't really know. But when my criminal injuries compensation finally comes through, I'm going to get my own place again. Maybe ask my brother Adam if he wants to share with me. I definitely want to live on my own again. I miss having my independence. Then I'll just carry on. I'm sure that one day I will be able to see again. I'm positive. You've got to have a positive mind, haven't you?

Lisa: Have you got a positive mind, Daniel? Do you feel positive about your life?

Daniel: Yeah. Yes. Definitely. I've got to be positive, if I'm not, then he may as well have killed me really.

Lisa: What about the media – they took up your story, didn't they?

Daniel: I had a little bit of interest. The *Western Daily Press*, and then I was in the *Sun* and *The Times*, but it wasn't real news interest, it was just page five or whatever.

Lisa: And were they knocking at your mum's door?

Daniel: Yeah, they . . . I think they actually came to the hospital and wanted to do the story then, but my mum thought she was going to lose me, that I was going to die, so she didn't want any press to get involved. Which is understandable, really.

I did get quite a lot of coverage during the first couple of years, just here and there. People started to recognise me. I'd be out in the street with Mum and she'd notice people looking at me as if they were thinking, 'Where have I seen that man before? Who is he?' And occasionally I'd get people coming up to me and saying, 'Oh hi, how are you? How's it going? I saw it in the paper. Excellent stuff. Good.' It was very odd, being recognised for what you did . . .

Lisa: And did you get any awards or anything? Did you go on television? Did you have any more news come round, when your court case came up?

Daniel: I've been on HTV and on the BBC, they've both come round and filmed me. Making a cup of tea, and walking down the street, things like that. I've been in all the newspapers. I was awarded the *Evening Post* Gold Star Award – in 1997 I think that was – which I thought was a really good thing to get, because it was a little gold and silver medal with a star in it. And I met a few celebrities there, like some of the local news presenters and people like that. I thought it was really good. I had a really nice day out, and a meal down at the Marriott Hotel in Bristol.

    And then I was given a Waley Cohen Award, which is the highest award the police give you. They gave me a certificate and a crystal vase – I thought it was very handy for a bloke to have a crystal vase! That was at Portishead Police Station, in early 1998 I think.

    I was happy that somebody had acknowledged what I'd done. It was nice to be recognised for doing that, rather than being swept under the carpet and forgotten about. It was good to feel that people acknowledged the fact that I did actually try to help somebody. And then there was the Pride of Britain Award.

Lisa: Oh yeah, which is where we met. When did you find out about that, then?

Daniel: The week before. Somebody from the *Daily Mirror* phoned up and said I'd been nominated for the Pride of Britain Award – I knew absolutely nothing about it, it was the first I'd ever heard of it. They told me that thousands of other people had been nominated as well, so don't hold your breath, whatever, you know. I said, 'Well it's nice to be nominated anyway.' I put the phone down, and then a week later they phoned me up again and said I'd actually won this award. Mel C – Scary Spice – she was the one who actually picked me out apparently.

They said I'd have to go up to London to receive it. They paid for our train tickets to London – I went with my mum and my brother Adam. They put us up at a really nice hotel in Kensington, which was rather plush. Then the next day a limo took us to the Dorchester. We arrived, and the press were all there. We had special passes to get in, which felt really strange, because I still didn't know how big it was going to be. We went in and they said we were going to meet the Prime Minister. I thought, 'What's going on here?' I met the Prime Minister and Cherie Blair, and Mo Mowlam was there. And the Queen of Jordan.

Lisa: Was it quite overwhelming?

Daniel: Slightly, yes. They put us on the top table, right at the front. I was next to Cilla Black. I asked her if I could come on *Blind Date* – which she thought was funny. There were a couple of newsreaders from ITN. They were brilliant. It was a very big occasion. I was escorted by Adam up this slope onto the stage to receive the award – and you were up there and presented it to me . . .

Lisa: I'd read all about you, and I thought, 'It's just amazing what he's been through.' And I could see Carol Vorderman was in tears when she was telling everyone what you had done and what had happened.

Daniel: And then Adam gave a little speech that I'd prepared for him. So he read this speech, and then he added a little bit on the end that he'd written himself, and it was – brilliant. The whole room stood up and gave us a standing ovation. People were in tears. It was quite emotional. I wish I could have seen as well as heard. There were so many unbelievable people there. And I was given a big glass plaque and a holiday to Minorca – which I'm yet to take. I'll take it next October. It's going to be in *OK!* magazine as well.

Lisa: And from there you got some more media attention as well, didn't you?

Daniel: Yes. On Monday after the awards Richard and Judy telephoned me and asked me to go on their show. So they sent me a couple of train tickets to go up to their show one afternoon. I went on the show and came home the same day.

I met Chris Evans, who invited me onto *TFI Friday*, which I went to three or four weeks ago. That was really good. They gave us a train ticket, put us up in a hotel on Friday night, so we went on the show in the afternoon. Free bar, obviously, while you are in the studio. We had 'Access' passes to all areas, so we could wander around and talk to everyone. I spoke to Chris several times, and he came out with us for a drink afterwards. It was un-believable. Went down to their local pub in the evening with them all, and chatted to whoever was there. Courtney Love was there, and People of the South played. Mel C was there again. Pretty good it was. Magic.

Lisa: You'll remember it for the rest of your life. Pity you had to go through all that just to get it, though.

Daniel: Exactly. I'd rather not have had any of it, just to be able to get on with my life the way I used to.

Lisa: Do you ever wish you could put the clock back?

Daniel: I'd give it all up if I could get my sight back. Not that I've got anything much to give up. I'm not exactly living in a huge mansion with a butler.

Lisa: So you'll go on holiday in Minorca – then what's going to happen, do you think?

Daniel: I honestly don't know. I'd like to go round schools and colleges and give talks on being disabled. I've done a bit of that already. At my old grammar school I went in and gave a few talks to the kids there, on various disabilities including blindness, and what it's like for wheelchair users. How you should treat a person with a disability. It's a worthwhile thing, I think, to help people become more aware about what it's like to be disabled.

I have a stick, but people don't always realise that I'm blind. My eyes are perfect – apart from the fact that I can't see, obviously! The fronts of my eyes are OK. People look at me and think, 'Why is that young man carrying a white stick?' You have to be a bit light-hearted about it.

Lisa: Have you anything else you want to say before we stop, Daniel?

Daniel: Tell them I'm twenty-four, I'm single, I'm really good-looking, so if there's anybody out there . . . (*Laughs*)

Lisa: (Laughs) I'll make sure there's a photo of you in the book.

Lisa's Reflections

Although what happened to Daniel was in May 1996, Daniel was the last of my 'heroes' that I actually met. That was in April 1999 at the *Mirror* Pride of Britain Awards.

I was presenting Daniel with the award for courage. It was so sad listening to his story as Carol Vorderman told it to us. And his brother Adam's speech was really hard-hitting about how unlucky Daniel had been. I thought, 'Goodness me. This lad is so young, and he was just trying to help someone and he's come away blinded and with such horrific injuries.' It made me think about how lucky I was.

When I was chatting to Daniel after the ceremony I asked him if he'd be in my book, because I thought it was important to show that heroes don't always come away from their adventures with a gold medal round their neck. Sometimes the hero ends up as the victim – and it's really surprising how little help there is for victims. Like Daniel, I don't know where I would have been without my mum. She did everything for me in the beginning, like Sylvia has for Daniel. And you have to rely so much on your family to get you through the first few months.

Families are often forgotten in all of this, and they suffer just as much. I know my mum and dad went through nights of worry at the beginning. Wishing they could have saved me.

I think Daniel is still feeling pretty numb compared with me, because he's still dealing with his physical injuries. He hasn't been able to move on to getting help with sorting out his emotional pain and psychological injuries. He has more or less shut everything down for now, which is exactly what I did for two years. He has to cope with something as big as losing his sight and also, as he said, it will take him five years to come completely out of the coma, which doesn't leave him with much heart to start facing any other problems.

I didn't feel ready to talk to anybody about my own angry feelings and depression for the first two years.

Trauma counsellors come in and help people straight after something like this, but at that point you probably only need to have a cup of tea with your mum, and talk to friends and close family. You don't want somebody then. It's later on when things start to settle down physically that psychologically it starts to drip out slowly. I think if we had to deal with everything at once our hearts and minds couldn't cope.

I didn't realise before talking to Daniel that it could take so long to come round from being in a coma. Like everyone else who watches television, with programmes like *Peak Practice* where you have a disaster but in the end everything's fine, I thought that that's how it is. But real life isn't at all like that. Daniel waking up and finding out that he couldn't see and that he was extremely ill – that's reality. Not, 'Hello, Mum. Yes, I'm fine now. We're all going to be happy.'

Another hard thing for Daniel is that nobody has ever thanked him for what he did. In my case, the children and their parents have all been so grateful and thanked me so much and so often, it's all been worth it. But nobody is grateful to Daniel. It was a case of thankless heroism. Of course his parents and brothers are proud of him, but there was something his mother said that I thought was nice, when she said that she had always been proud of him – before all this happened. She said he'd been brave all his life. I'm sure she wishes that Daniel had never had anything to do with this particular incident. In fact, she said to me later that if something like this ever happened again and Daniel looked as though he was going to help, she would personally shoot him!

The struggle doesn't ever seem to end. Three and a half years down the line and I'm still waiting for my own criminal injuries compensation, and Daniel is in the same boat. People find it hard to believe. You go through all of that, and then you have to wait and wait for your money for all the injuries you've received. It stops you from getting on with life. I know it does with me, because I think, 'Well once that's come through, once I know what it is, then I can plan where I'm going to go and what I'm going to do. Then I can put all those folders away, and not have to look at them again for years and years to come.' That's something I do get fed up about – and that's a part of Daniel's story that I can really relate to, waiting for life to begin again, for the chance to regain his independence.

Another thing he's had to endure that I know very well is having to go along to outpatients three times a week for occupational therapy and physiotherapy. I had to do it for two years to help regain the use of my left hand. After two years I stopped for a bit, then I had an operation and then I had to go back again. Those things are forgotten, and you just have to get on with it, but it could easily make you bitter that someone caused you all that trouble.

Where Daniel is different from me is that he, for understandable reasons, really regrets doing what he did. For him, it wasn't worth it. I can't say that. I don't know how I would feel if I'd been injured as seriously as Daniel was, and gone blind. I suppose that would have made me more angry and bitter. But I would still feel that I was glad that I had done what I did and that it was worthwhile, because all those children are alive and happy today. Of course I would give anything for the man never to have attacked and harmed them – but I don't think I would ever regret having tried to stop him.

It's going to take a long time, but Daniel has got the determination to come through this. That's what I liked about him, his great spirit and hopefulness. The last thing he wants is for people to say, 'Oh, poor Daniel.' He is even positive about his blindness and really believes that – one day – technology will help him to see again. He's got the support of a family who love him very much. He's a young man with a lot to give, a great sense of humour, a lovely personality and once he has healed a bit more I really hope that his story will have a happy ending.

5

Karen and Darren Howells – The Good Neighbours

Southampton

May 1997

Karen and Darren Howells are a young couple that anyone would want as their neighbours. They used their instinct to act quickly in an emergency, and saved a life just as surely as anyone else in this book, although they didn't have to confront any actual danger. In their story, a frightened and very ill old lady telephoned them late one evening by mistake, because she had got the wrong number. They followed it up, discovered who she was and where she lived, and stayed with her until an ambulance came.

I met Karen and Darren at the People of the Year Awards in November 1997. It was actually Karen alone who got the People of the Year Award, as though Darren had had nothing to do with it. I think that was because Karen had had all the press and media attention earlier on, because Darren was always at work – and she is a lovely, bright and chatty young girl, so the press loved her.

So when I went to interview them at their home in Southampton Karen said, 'Before you put on the tape, I've got to tell you something . . . It wasn't just me who was in this story. Darren played a big part in it, so I want it to be both of us, in your book. Because he's never had any appreciation for it.'

So this is how they told me their story between them.

Karen and Darren's Story

Lisa: *Karen is five foot, very petite, with honey-blonde hair.*

Karen: I'd say ginger!

Lisa: *No, honey-blonde. Blue eyes, long eyelashes, fragile, very pretty. You can describe Darren. I don't want to describe your man!*

Karen: Darren is six foot, has lovely curly hair, quite broad, and all in proportion. I think he's quite slim – I don't see him as fat, anyway. Green eyes.

I'm twenty-six years old. I'm a secretary in a roofing company. Darren and I have been married now for just over a year, and we were engaged and lived together for about two years before that.

Darren: I'm thirty-two. I'm a van driver and I work for a kitchen worktop specialist.

Karen: It was the first Bank Holiday Monday in May 1997, so it was 5 May. It was a beautiful day, sunny and hot. We had been to a barbecue at Darren's youngest brother, who lived round the corner from us. We came home at about half past nine in the evening. We were relaxing in front of the TV and Darren had just come in with the coffee, when the telephone rang. It was between half nine and ten o'clock. Quite late, and if a friend telephones it's normally before then, so we thought it was a bit unusual. Darren answered it.

Darren: It was a wrong number. I could hear an old lady on the other end of the line, sounding distressed, and she was asking for 'Mary'. She sounded very upset and a bit confused. I said there was no Mary here. I asked her if she was OK, but she kept on asking for Mary. I said, 'Are you sure you are OK?'

She said, 'Yes, I just want my friend.' And she hung up. So I called Karen.

Karen: He came in from the hall and told me about it, and said she sounded very upset, and that he was worried. So we decided to do 1471 to get her number, and I called her back. When she picked up the telephone I could tell from her voice that she'd been crying. She sounded terribly worried.

I explained to her that she had rung our number by mistake. I asked her if she was OK, and she said, no, she had a terrible pain in her stomach. I asked her if she'd like us to come round, and she said yes. She gave us her address. I think she was not in her right state of mind at all. So we thought this was the best thing to do, to go round to see for ourselves.

Lisa: Darren, what made you – because most people would just say, 'Sorry, love, no Mary lives here, goodbye' – what made you say to Karen 'I think we should do something about this'?

Darren: I don't know. We've had wrong numbers before, when I've just said, 'Sorry, mate, wrong number'. But I've

99

never before heard anyone sound so frightened. And she was obviously an old lady. I don't know. I've got an old grandmother. I would do the same for her if need be. I don't know. I just thought we should find out, really. Which is why I asked Karen to ring her back. I thought if she heard a bloke telephoning her, she might get frightened.

Karen: I said to her that we could come round and help her. She put the telephone down saying, 'Please hurry.' So we knew we had to get there pretty quick. Darren got his road-map out and we realised she lived literally five minutes down the road, which was very lucky, so we left everything and drove straight down there. My full cup of coffee was just left! We ran out of the house. It was quite late by then, I always remember, because I had my summer dress on and it was freezing. But we didn't think, we just ran out of the door and drove straight there.

Lisa: You could have thought, 'Well, whatever the matter is, it's nothing to do with us.' And left it at that.

Karen: We couldn't have slept that night if we'd done that. We'd both have worried about her. I needed to know for myself that she was all right.

Darren: We did think at the time, maybe we will be interfering, but we couldn't have just let it go. She was obviously trying to get hold of her friend Mary but for some reason, either by bad luck or good luck, she got in touch with us instead. It turned out later that Mary only lived a few doors away, and her number was very similar to ours. It was just one digit different.

Lisa: So you dashed off like Starsky and Hutch in the car – and got to the house?

Karen: Yes. She lived in a large complex of warden-assisted flats. So we rushed around, trying to find her. Eventually we found the flat upstairs, knocked on the door, and I shouted through the letterbox who I was.

Darren: We were trying to find a warden first of all, but we couldn't. We searched through the whole complex to find a warden. But then we found the old lady's flat, and that's when we knocked on the door.

Lisa: Did she open the door?

Karen: No. So I banged on the door, and said, 'It's the lady you spoke to on the telephone. Can I come in?'
    And she said, 'Yes. It's open.'
    So I opened the door – I didn't have a clue what I was going to walk into. Darren stayed outside in case the warden came. I don't think anything was going through my mind except wondering what I was going to see.
    She was slumped on her chair in her nightie, very poorly and very upset and confused. She didn't really know where she was. She told me her name, which is Vera. She said she had a bad stomach and had been sick. So I helped to tidy her up and cleaned her up.

Lisa: She'd been sick?

Karen: Yes, she'd brought up something or other, so I went in to her kitchen . . .

Lisa: But you didn't know this lady . . . and you just went to her kitchen and you cleaned up her sick for her?

Karen: Yes, I found something to wipe her down.

Lisa: You shouldn't be a secretary — you're a Florence Nightingale.

Karen: No, no, not really. I just wiped her down and put her nightie straight. You know, that's not much to do . . .

Lisa: Was the telly on?

Karen: No, she was just sitting in her chair, and she was slumped in it, deathly white. She was very shaken because she didn't know what had happened to her. I found an intercom cord in her flat, so I called that and spoke to a central control, and said, please could they get an ambulance. They said a doctor would be on his way, and we had to wait for the doctor.

Lisa: Were you comforting the lady?

Karen: Yes, I put my arm round her. I asked her if she had any family. She had a daughter but she didn't live nearby. I tried to reassure her more than anything else, and tried to make her forget her pain. She was holding her stomach. We didn't really talk very much, we were just anxious for someone to come and help her more than anything.

Lisa: And where were you at the time, Darren?

Darren: I waited downstairs, because Karen told me there was a doctor on the way. So I was looking out for someone to turn up. When he arrived I showed him to the flat. He asked Karen to leave then because he had to examine her, and so we went out. A few of the neighbours were beginning to come out of their flats to see what was going on.

Lisa: *How long had you been in the flat before the doctor came?*

Karen: About fifteen minutes. It was some time after ten when he came.

Lisa: *And in that fifteen minutes you became quite friendly with this lady, who wasn't your own grandma? And you'd cleaned up her sick and been really nice to her?*

Karen: She was a dear old soul. I was worried for her more than anything. To see somebody, an older person, in that state, is really upsetting.

When the doctor arrived I explained that we didn't know this lady, that really she'd got hold of us by mistake, but we'd come round and found her in this state.

He wasn't at all interested in that, and asked me what medication she was on. I didn't have a clue. I went into the kitchen where I'd seen some tablets, and got them for him. He then asked me to leave while he examined her.

I think what annoyed me more than anything was his attitude . . . it was probably because it was a Bank Holiday, and it was getting quite late. Time was getting on a bit. He was not interested in who I was, or in the old lady in her chair . . .

Darren: He was a bit miffed at being called out . . .

Karen: Yeah, that's the impression we got. I know it's an awful thing to say, but that's totally the impression he made. As though we were just a nuisance.

I waited outside with Darren while he examined her. He finished the examination, let me back in, left me with a note and her tablets in a bag and asked me to keep it and wait with her until the ambulance arrived. He had called the ambulance from Vera's flat. So he just left this stuff with us, and said the ambulance would be along shortly. And that was it. He left.

Lisa: Was she still in pain? Did she say what the doctor had said?

Karen: At this point she was on the sofa, not the chair. I got her dressing gown and put it round her, then I sat down beside her and put my arms around her. Then two of her friends – Dot and the one she'd been trying to telephone, Mary – arrived because they'd heard a commotion and come in to see what was the matter. We explained to them what had happened. And they got her things together for hospital. Darren was outside looking out for the ambulance. He went downstairs to guide them up to the flat.

Lisa: Did her friends think you were her granddaughter or something?

Karen: No, they knew Vera and her family, so they knew we were complete strangers.

Lisa: Were you stressed by any of this, or were you calm?

Karen: No, I was completely calm. I can get flustered, but I don't think you do at the time, you just go with the flow. I went along with the situation as it unfolded. I felt completely calm . . . I don't know how you felt, Darren?

Darren: Cold! I was outside waiting for the ambulance, because it was quite a large area of sheltered accommodation, and I wanted to make sure he came in the right end of it.

I knew Karen was a decent, chatty person who could keep Vera's mind off her troubles. And now her friends were there too, she would see people she recognised.

Lisa: *You talk about Vera as though she were your own grannie!*

Darren: She almost is now. She's become like a surrogate grandmother.

Lisa: *Did she smile at her friends? Did she know them?*

Karen: No, not really. I think she was still in too much pain. She really wasn't quite with it. She knew who her friends were, but she didn't say, 'Oh thank God you're here.' I think she felt so dreadfully poorly, she just wanted to get to hospital.

Then the ambulance men arrived, after about another ten, fifteen minutes. They came in, wrapped her up, I gave them the letter and tablets and asked if she was going to be OK. They said she'd be fine. I asked where she was going to be taken, and we did offer to go with her, but the ambulance men said, no, she'd be OK. The friends walked down to the ambulance with us. Then they took her away, and we stood there with her friends for another twenty minutes, talking to them about everything that had happened.

I think they were quite in shock that it was two young people who had done this. Obviously it was an old people's complex, and they all rather had the attitude 'Young people today . . .' So I think they were surprised that we were young people who had gone out of their way to help someone.

Then we drove home, at about half past eleven, and our cups of stone-cold coffee were still sitting there. We went straight up to bed because we had to go to work the next day. Then we were lying in bed and our heads were just buzzing with what had happened. We were awake for about an hour talking about it all and asking each other, 'Do you think she'll be all right?'

Darren: We were glad we had followed it through and that she was safely in hospital – I don't mean pleased with ourselves, but just glad that we had been able to help, rather than just hang up.

Lisa: Did you feel special? Did you think 'That's really nice what we've just done. Aren't we nice people?'

Karen: No! (*Laughs*) Even now, we don't think we've done anything that's such a big deal, and then we certainly didn't. Not until people started to say that what we'd done was really good.

Lisa: So then what happened?

Karen: Woke up the next morning, went to work. As soon as I got in I telephoned the hospital. The ambulance men had told us which hospital she was being taken to.

I explained that I'd been with Vera the night before. The nurse said that because I wasn't family, she couldn't tell me anything apart from the fact that she'd been operated on that night.

That left me in a complete panic, thinking, 'Oh my goodness, what's wrong?'

Lisa: A complete panic? But you didn't even know this lady . . .

Karen: I know, but I was really worried, wondering what was wrong with her. I called Darren. We were left in the dark, and it was awful, not knowing all that day and all the next day. We kept ringing the hospital to find out how she was, but they couldn't tell us anything.

You couldn't go through something like that and just leave it. You have to know what happened next. How could you help someone and then just think, 'Oh, well, that's it.' You need to know the end, don't you? You need to know how things turn out.

Lisa: Oh sure. So two days went by without you knowing anything at all?

Karen: Well, we knew she was all right by then, they told us that much, but not what had been the matter, and what the operation was for. On the Tuesday and the Wednesday after the Bank Holiday we didn't hear anything. It must have been the Thursday morning, just before I went to work, that I had a phone call from Janet Browning, who is Vera's daughter, thanking us for helping her mother.

Lisa: How did she get your number?

Karen: From Mary, the friend, because we'd discussed the fact that our number was just one digit different from hers. Janet told me that Vera had had a perforated ulcer, and that she was still quite poorly. I don't know if she could have died or not. I think she could have, possibly, if we hadn't got there when we did and rushed things along.

Lisa: Was she thankful, the daughter?

Karen: She was wonderful, absolutely wonderful. Very thankful to us both, and we went through the whole story and told her everything that had happened, because at that stage, she didn't really know. I said, 'Could we come along to the hospital to see Vera?' She said she was still very poorly, but she would let me know what was going on, and would like to meet up with us. Then Janet called again over the weekend as well, just to say how Vera was.

Lisa: *Were you quite looking forward to seeing Vera again?*

Karen: Yes, I was. I still had that mental picture of her slumped over her chair, deathly pale, the way I'd found her – and I wanted to see her looking better again. I just needed to get rid of that other picture. It had stayed with me a bit, and I needed to see that she was OK for myself. It's OK people telling you, but you want to see for yourself.

Lisa: *What did you do at the weekend?*

Darren: Nothing extraordinary. A bit of decorating, I've no doubt. Just the usual things. I was asking Karen about Vera. She spoke to Janet.

Karen: The following week we had a message on the answer machine from the *Southampton Daily Echo* saying that somebody had nominated me for the Bouquet of the Week because of what had happened to Vera. And they said they'd like to do the story as well, and would I like to meet up with them at the Southampton General Hospital – this was all on the answer machine – and was I interested in doing the story, and could I get back to somebody.

Lisa: *What did you think when you listened to that message?*

Darren: I think we just thought, 'Oh my God.'

Lisa: Didn't they offer Darren a bouquet of flowers? Did you want one?

Darren: Yeah, or maybe a crate of beer . . . But it was all directed more towards Karen, because Karen was the one Mary had talked to, and it was through Mary that the *Echo* got in touch with us.

Karen: It was quite exciting at first. This sort of thing doesn't happen to us. I felt quite nervous. So I rang them back and said it would be very nice, the bouquet, and I would agree to meet them at the hospital, but only if Janet said that it was OK. Because obviously if Vera was too poorly, there was no way it was going to happen.

Darren: All you really wanted to do was to go and see Vera, didn't you? You didn't really want the *Echo* to be there. You just wanted to see how she was, and to meet Janet.

Karen: Yes, I would have preferred it if I could have seen her on my own first of all, to be honest. Rather than having a reporter and a photographer there, the first time you meet somebody. That was a bit awkward, so it was like you were a star or something when you come in.

That was the Tuesday. We agreed to meet on the Wednesday, all of us including Darren. But unfortunately I couldn't get hold of Darren in time, because he was working in Poole, and his boss wouldn't give me his phone number on the site, so I went with my mum in the end.

Lisa: Were you quite nervous?

Karen: Completely terrified. I was a bag of nerves. I can remember rushing around quickly getting ready, picking up my mum. I needed someone there to support me. We drove up to the hospital, and there were a photographer and a couple of journalists. All I can remember is walking in the room and completely blanking these people, and rushing straight up to Vera in her bed. We were both quite emotional. She was crying and I was crying. It was really lovely to see her, bless her. And then I met her daughter, Janet. And obviously then, I had to do the interview.

Lisa: What did Vera say to you when you went over to her?

Karen: What she always says . . . oh, it's really embarrassing . . . 'You are my angel.' I just went over and gave her a big hug, and we were both very tearful. Of course she was still very poorly.

Lisa: Did she say, 'You saved my life'?

Karen: She always says that! I find it difficult to acknowledge that. We just don't see it like that. We didn't feel we did anything special, did we?

Darren: It's all down to your instincts, how an individual reacts at the time.

Lisa: No, but to her, you did. To her you are really special because you saved her life.

Karen: I don't know. Anyway, we were both completely soppy. And her daughter was completely wonderful. And then basically I was pounced on by the *Echo*. My mum sat chatting to Janet, while Vera and I had loads of photographs done. I didn't enjoy that at all. I don't like having my picture taken anyway, but this poor lady had been really ill, and they don't just take one or two photos, they take hundreds. I thought it was too much of an ordeal. I didn't think it was fair. They had me kneeling on the floor and all sorts – it was just too much. Then we did an interview, and I explained the situation. I think Darren did get his name mentioned somewhere in there!

Lisa: *So next day – it was in the* Echo?

Karen: Front page! Huge headlines. Something like 'Life Saver'. And another one was 'Good Samaritans', with a photo of Vera and me. I remember I was at work and saying to someone, 'Oh, it might be in the *Echo*, would you pick us one up?'

And he came back with four, and said, 'You're front page.'

And I completely freaked out. I thought, 'Oh my God – what do I look like?'

I was so embarrassed. Especially, I remember buying a copy of the *Echo* and the woman served me and went, 'That's you.' I went bright red. And it was quite embarrassing with all our friends.

Some people did get jealous. I remember one person in particular saying, 'Yeah, I did see it, but I didn't like to buy it.' Now, if it was one of my friends I'd say, 'Wow! My friend is there.' And I'd have bought it. But sometimes you do get a bit of jealousy. So people reacted differently. Most people were really pleased for us.

Lisa: *And did you get the Bouquet of the Week?*

Karen: No! I didn't. The Bouquet of the Week didn't make the front page. So that week it went to someone else.

Darren: I read the *Echo* that night. I read the report, and it said 'Karen's Fiancé – see page 11.' So I flicked to page 11 just to see my name! I'm that sad! It was just my name: Darren helps, van driver. It didn't bother me, it made me laugh.

Lisa: And seeing Karen on the front page – did that seem strange?

Darren: It was like another stage – from being phoned up by the *Echo* about the flowers, to being on the front page. It was like increasing, every time. And yes, it did seem strange.

Karen: You remember what you did? You went round to the local newsagents. And you know how they have the big white posters in the windows? He got it.

Darren: It said, 'Good Samaritan saves lives'. I went in and said to the girl behind the counter, 'Do you mind if I take your poster? That's my girlfriend.' She didn't say anything, so I just took it down and walked out.

Lisa: Did you feel proud of her?

Darren: Yes, of course I did. Very, very much so. I was involved in it, but I wasn't given the publicity, but at least I knew somebody who was. I was pleased that at least one of us was getting recognition for it. That makes me sound bitter and twisted! But it was nice to hear, whenever she popped back from the shops, that people were stopping her in Tescos.

Karen: Yeah. Mainly older people, who'd seen me in the paper, would stop me and say, 'Oh, what you did was really good.' I was a bit embarrassed, but I just sort of thanked them.

What we often got was people saying, 'Other people wouldn't have done that. You know, we'd have ignored it.'

And I say, 'But would you?'

And they say, 'Yes, I'd have ignored it.' But I don't know.

Lisa: After going round interviewing lots of different people, I've found that it is about people's characters. Something inside, I think it's something to do with the way a person is.

Karen: Yeah, well I think we are both quite caring people, aren't we? We do care about people. There are people out there who just care about themselves. That's fine, but we are not like that. And a lot of our friends aren't like that. They do worry about others, which I think is a good thing.

That evening the telephone didn't stop ringing. We had *Bella* magazine, Radio Solent, Radio Five, so then my husband – boyfriend at that time – who had really been just as much a part of it as I was, had to be my agent, taking all these calls! Darren would say, 'So and so wants to speak to you.'

I began thinking, 'Oh, leave me alone!'

I did the radio interviews. And *Bella* magazine, and then all of a sudden it was as if every magazine was ringing up. But you have to sign a contract with *Bella* to say that you won't sell the story to anyone else until they've published it. So that did put quite a lot of them off, because we had quite a few, didn't we, ringing up?

And then it went into the *Daily Mail.* I had the *Mail* reporter. Then it went into the *Sun* and the *Mirror.* For a couple of days it all went mad.

I just kept thinking, 'I can't keep taking all this time off work to have my photo taken!' I was trying to go to work, nine to five, normal person, but I'd get all these people phoning me up at work. I don't know how they got the number. Wanting to interview me, do photos.

We then had Meridian, the local TV station, on the phone. They have a nightly news programme at six o'clock, and they wanted to interview both of us for it. But once again, Darren could not get the time off work. So I had to re-enact the situation on my own. A film crew came back to my house and interviewed me about what had happened. I then had to go round to Vera's and re-enact the situation there, running down the road. It was awful.

The people at my work were wonderful. They just said, 'You enjoy your fifteen minutes of fame. Just go and take it.'

Lisa: Is that what it felt like, fifteen minutes of fame?

Karen: Yes. After the *Echo* I had really thought it would stop. But it didn't, it just escalated more and more. And when it got to the point that my family couldn't get through on the phone for all these journalists, I thought, 'I've had enough now.' I'd had enough after three or four days of being pulled around. I just think, you are the story of the moment, and they want it. They don't care about you. They don't care about the situation. It's just, 'I want the story, and then I'm going.' Because that's their job, isn't it?

Darren: I was answering the phone all the time. I couldn't think what the fuss was about. It was no big deal. I didn't understand it. I still don't. It seemed to have been blown up so much, it was just snowballing, and it carried on and on.

Karen: Every single paper got the story slightly wrong. None of them got it completely right, did they? It was quite frustrating, because I'd think, 'But I didn't say that. It wasn't like that.' Sometimes they put it in a way you wish they hadn't, and I did find it a bit cringe-making.

And when we did the TV, they actually did a link-up with Janet that evening. I didn't see it until it came on that night. I hid behind a pillow, thinking how awful I looked. And they had also interviewed Vera to say how she felt. She said on TV that she was very grateful to Karen *and* Darren.

Lisa: Great double act: Karen and Darren. So how did you feel, when she said she was grateful to you both?

Karen: She is just so wonderful, whenever I see her I want to grab her and hug her and cry. It just upsets me – every time. I'm such a wimp. It just pulls at my heart strings, that's all. It isn't that it's sad.

And then Vera came on the *Bella* magazine shoot as well. That was awful, because we were out there for about two hours in the sun. Vera was eighty-eight then. It was too much to put her through. And Janet, her daughter, said, 'It's got to stop now, because it's not fair.'

But in a way it was great for Vera, because she had her bit of limelight. She was eighty-eight, and suddenly she had family getting in touch that she'd lost contact with, and friends she hadn't seen in years saw her picture in the paper and wrote to her again. Which was brilliant.

After about a week things went back to normal. And that was it. I mean still occasionally people would stop me, like the girl in the post office would say, 'I've just seen you in this magazine' or whatever. Little mentions went on appearing here and there.

Lisa: What about your parents, how did they react?

Karen: I think my dad bought about four copies of everything!

Lisa: Ah! Bless him. Like my dad. He was exactly the same. My dad came back and he said, 'Ah! My Lisa's in the paper!'
Even after three years he still does it. I say, 'Oh shut up. I'm boring.'
But it's still, 'Our Lisa's on the telly!'
To Vera that day, you were, to her, like somebody sent from somewhere. Do you have a faith? Are you religious at all? Do you believe in God?

Karen: No. I don't know. Maybe then I did, but not now. I find this very hard. So many bad things have happened to us recently, it makes me angry, and I think, 'If there is a God up there, how could you do this to us?' My granddad just recently passed away, and he suffered to the very end. Now that gets to you, because I loved him so dearly, and he suffered very badly. I get a bit bitter. So I don't know. At the moment I would say not. We're still getting over a sad situation. I just don't know.
I do think things happen for a reason. But I don't think I believe in a God.

Lisa: After that week, did you see Vera again?

Karen: After she came out of hospital her daughter took her away to Gloucester to stay with her for a few weeks to recuperate. When she brought her home, we both went round there to see her, didn't we? That was the first time for quite a long while, and the first time Darren had seen her since the first day, because he didn't come to the hospital.

Darren: I don't think she knew who I was, because that evening was a blur for her. It still is. She doesn't remember that evening at all.

Karen: She doesn't remember me either, on that evening. She remembers nothing.

Lisa: *Was that strange, going back to the house?*

Karen: It was just the same, but this time she looked lovely. She was healthy, and that made all the difference. She's got this lovely, thick white hair that anyone would die for, she's got beautiful hair. She's a very elegant woman. She's not a scrawny grandmother, and not a great fat one. She's just sort of medium. We adore her, don't we?

Lisa: *And then you got the People of the Year Award in November 1997. How did that come about?*

Karen: I've got absolutely no idea. I just got this letter from Radar saying I'd been nominated for a Person of the Year Award. I must admit, I was really chuffed. I was pleased, but I've got to say, again, that Darren's name wasn't on it. It does take that excitement off, because I feel like I'm taking it away from him, and we can't enjoy it together. That's difficult, but I discussed it with Darren. I'd never have accepted it without him agreeing, and he said, 'Yeah. Brilliant. Just go for it.'

And then our local *Echo* must have heard about it, and also Meridian found out. There was another piece in the *Echo*, and then we both did an interview with Meridian Television, didn't we?

Darren: Yes, I got roped into that one. There was no escape. But it was short and sweet.

Karen: And then we went to London in the November for the award. Everybody was so nice, weren't they? And Darren was included, he wasn't left out, which was nice, because unlike me he's quite shy, aren't you? And we met Moira Stewart, and she was wonderful, and she was so – well, just normal.

Lisa: Did you feel odd, meeting all these famous people, and wonder what you were doing there?

Karen: Yeah, it was really strange. They got Moira to come over and talk to us, and she stayed for ages, she's such a genuine person. And who else did we meet? Bert Massey, the director of RADAR, where all the money goes to, for charity. And Chris – he's Lord Tugendhat – is the chairman of Abbey National, and he was really nice, too. Everybody was.

Lisa: You walk in, don't you, with all the trumpeters playing?

Karen: I'm thinking, 'I'm going to trip or something' and Andy Keast of the British Lions rugby team said he was going to trip me up just as I walked in the door, so I remember being in hysterics as I was walking through. I was very nervous. I was frantically looking for Darren. I had to see his face. You've got all these people staring at you. How I got through that meal, I don't know. I could feel it just sliding down my throat.

It appeared in *The Times* a couple of days later, and you were in the paper the same day on a different page with your George Medal. And I thought, 'I've met her!'

Lisa: *And then did life go back to normal?*

Karen: I think it was in the paper again a couple of days after the award ceremony, and on the television they'd linked up and showed me walking up on the stage. So when we got back that night, a couple of neighbours called round, and we got a few notes through the door from people saying, 'Oh, we've seen you on TV! Well done. That was wonderful!' And at the end of that year the *Echo* did something in the paper about events that happened that year, and I was in the centre page. So again, people were saying, 'Oh, I saw you in the *Echo*.' Strangers in the street, and a lot of older people have stopped me to say things like, 'We didn't know there were people like you around anymore . . .'

Lisa: *Has it affected you emotionally at all?*

Karen: I don't know. I don't think so. What do you think?

Darren: You always seem to get emotional every time we go to see Vera . . .

Karen: Oh yes. Every time I see Vera, that's it, I do cry. Oh dear, yes. She is now like a grandmother to us, isn't she? She is so adorable. All she ever does is kiss us and thank us. She lives with her daughter now, so we don't see her so often. As a person, she is doing so well, she's ninety and she's going to outlive us all, I think.

Lisa: *Would you have changed anything you did that day?*

Darren: No, I don't think so. It all turned out right in the end.

Lisa's Reflections

What I really love about this story is the fact that young people very often don't get much praise or credit for caring about other people. A lot of young people are very kind and caring, but older people sometimes seem to think we are all selfish. When Vera telephoned that night, Darren could easily just have said, 'Sorry, love, wrong number' and hung up.

(It's quite amazing, that 1471 number you can do now. Every time you see a play on television, when someone picks up the telephone just as it stops ringing, you think, 'Try 1471!')

Karen and Darren said that so many people had admitted to them that they didn't think they would have done it. They would just have put the phone down and gone back to watching the telly. But how can you know? Until you are put into the situation. People often say that to me, 'Oh I could never have done what you did.'

And I say, 'You don't know. Until you are in that situation you can never tell.' But of course, it is true that a lot of people don't want to get involved, and wouldn't have done what Karen and Darren did.

It's an instinctive act. It's like, 'Oh my gosh, this is happening. I've got to do something quick.' Like so many people in this book, Karen and Darren did just that, or in her words, 'You just go with the flow.' That's what all my heroes have in common. They don't think about the washing they've left on the line or that they've left things in the sink, or the television programme they want to watch. They just think, 'I've got to go out there and do this.' That's why Karen left her coffee and went out in just her summer dress, even though it was cold and late at night.

Another thing I like about this story is little details like when she told me, 'Darren got his road-map out.' Darren did all the practical things, got out his map, found the way, drove the car, waited for the doctor and the ambulance to show them the way. Karen did all the loving, nurturing things, cleaned up the sick, and put her arm round Vera and comforted her.

And they didn't just help on the spur of the moment, and then that was it. They went on caring and worrying about what had happened to Vera and phoning up the hospital. What is sweet is how emotional Karen gets about Vera, and really wanting to see her again, to see for herself that she was all right. That's what happened to me, with the children, because I kept thinking I really wanted to see them again, see that they hadn't been too badly hurt. I needed to see them looking how they used to look, but sadly for me I never have seen that, because they've got facial scars.

Vera always says to Karen, 'You're my angel.' I loved hearing that. I told them how they'd put on the front of one of the newspapers in my case, 'Angel of St Luke's' and my dad used to say, 'An angel? You!' And you know yourself, it isn't true, that you have tantrums and behave badly like everybody else a lot of the time. I said, 'Little do they know that you are not really an angel!' And Darren was laughing.

And I quite understand how it makes Karen cry when she sees Vera. I got a little plaque from one of the children when I left the school and it said, 'Thank you for saving my life.' It was the worst thing ever and tears just poured down my face. It's something that just pulls at your heartstrings. It makes your heart feel like it's ripped out on the floor. I was so glad Karen felt like that, too. It makes you feel there is someone who understands. I really hope that Karen and Darren will always be my friends now.

I think in a way it's because Karen and Darren are such

caring people, who obviously love their own grandparents very much, that they find it difficult to believe in God. Because they want to do their utmost to make things come right for the people they love, they can't believe in a God who seems to allow things to happen. It's amazing, when sad things happen in your life, how much you can doubt. And I think it's only right to be allowed to doubt.

They really made an excellent team. I've got male and female heroes in my book, but Karen and Darren did it together. And although Karen more or less took over once they got there, Darren wasn't saying, 'Let's go home now. The doctor's coming. She'll be all right.' Which I'm sure a lot of people – men or women – might have done. Karen and Darren both cared, and saw it through to the end.

6

Graham Dennett
– The 'Pinball Wizard'

Car out of control on A55 westbound – the Conwy Tunnel

27 October 1995

This story is the tale of a real 'macho' man. It was a supreme case of someone being the right person in the right place at the right time when Graham Dennett prevented what might have been a major disaster. I went to see him at his home near Warrington.

Graham's Story

I'm forty-seven years old. What do I do? As little as possible for as much as possible! No, my business these days is putting gaming-machine operations in pubs and clubs. I travel in the northwest. Manchester, Liverpool, and down to North Wales, the camps, the caravan parks and various other sites down there.

I live in Warrington, Cheshire, in a little place called

Appleton Thorn. A bit of history here, we have 'bowling the thorn' – there is a thorn tree where you come in at the top, we have all the kids dancing round, and they tie ribbons on the trees. I've lived in and around Warrington all my life, but I've only lived in my present house for about two years.

There are quite a lot of us in the family, my parents and two sisters. Then I have several nephews and nieces. I've never had the courage to get married myself yet – never been that brave. Perhaps I will when I get to about sixty or seventy. I think twenty years is long enough to live with one person, and they say that we're all going to live to be ninety or a hundred nowadays!

After I left school I joined the police. I was in the police service for six years, until 1975, and then I became self-employed, and have been self-employed ever since. Doing various things – industrial cleaning company, haulage company, and now I'm just down to these gaming-machines operations.

On this particular day in October 1995 I'd been working in Warrington and in the afternoon I was taking some equipment to a caravan I have in North Wales, some pipe work and bits of pieces in the back of my truck, which is a four-wheel drive pick-up truck.

I was driving down the A55 towards North Wales, on the westbound carriageway, and was just approaching the Conwy Tunnel. There was very little traffic on the road, I seem to remember, and there was a small Citroen-type thing about a hundred or two hundred yards in front of me. It was either a Peugeot or a Citroen – one of those small, two-door saloons.

It would be doing about seventy miles an hour. It swung left. Then it swung to the right, and hit the central reservation, and gave it a glancing blow. It was a dual carriageway with crash barriers on the central reservation and there were grass banks on the side of the road.

Then it went back across the carriageway and all the way up the grass bank on the other side. High up the bank, round the back of one of the big road signs. You know the massive big signs telling you where you are going? It went all the way round the back of that, and then back down the bank and across the carriageway until it hit the central crash barrier again – this time very hard. Not quite at 90 degrees, more a 45-degree glancing blow, and hard, because he was still travelling fast. And then it carried on more or less in the right direction for a bit.

I thought it was very odd. The car didn't stop or slow down at all, it just kept going. I thought, 'There's something really weird about this.' It had been a fine day. The road wasn't wet. It was early evening time, just on the edge of dark – well, it was dark. I followed the car up, and he started to slow down a little now, so both our speeds were something in the region of sixty miles an hour. He was still going along keeping more or less on the tarmac, but a bit erratically. He was weaving around on the road.

I could see more traffic was coming down behind us, travelling faster than we were, and nobody else would know what was happening ahead, because it was only me who had seen him. So I had then to stop cars from passing – I had to use my vehicle to stop cars from overtaking, in case he swerved into them and caused a crash. So I was weaving from side to side. Some of them were getting quite annoyed then, and started to try and overtake on the inside. So I managed to stop that, until one other driver realised what was happening as well, so he stayed in the left-hand lane and I stayed in the right hand lane, and we stayed behind this car, as it was weaving its way into the Conwy Tunnel.

We followed him into the Tunnel, and he'd slowed down to about fifty miles an hour. I was very curious by then as to what was going on. I decided to move forward alongside him and try to get a look inside the car. I had it in my mind that the fellow was very, very drunk, because he'd just carried on driving. Drunk drivers have been known to hit something, and just carry on driving because they are not even aware of what they've done.

So he was swinging from one side of the road to the other as he went into the tunnel, but at a regular frequency, so when he'd gone over to one side, I decided to pull alongside of him and see what was going on. As I drove up beside him, I looked in and he was behind the wheel with his head back and he was like blowing vomit and bubbles and things through his mouth and nose. He was unconscious. And when I looked across even further, there was a young kid on the passenger seat, strapped into a baby seat, a little dark-haired lad. I always remember he was straining up, looking up at his dad or whoever the man was. I could see this kid's terrified face.

So then I thought, 'You're going to have do something here, Dennett. There's only you to do something about this.' So I thought I'd better try to push him sideways into the wall, to slow him down. Only I'd just had the truck repainted, and spent £1,000 on it, so I thought, 'No, I won't do that, I'll get in front of him, and catch him on the back of the truck.'

So that's what I did. I manoeuvred in front of him. I was in danger of running into the wall myself now, because I was looking back at him, to try and manoeuvre him onto the tow-bar at the back of the truck. Then I just hit the speed, and caught him up on the back of the truck and then braked slowly until we stopped. Then I got out and dashed back to his car to turn his engine off, because it was obviously racing away furiously.

He'd quite extensively damaged his front wing and the door, which had jammed, but fortunately his window was a little bit open, and I managed to get my hand in and jam it down and switch off his ignition. Then I realised that there was another child in the back seat. These two little children didn't make a sound. They just looked frozen with fear. Then I tried to get the door open, so I could pull his head forward to stop him choking. I knew he had to breathe – he was gurgling and going blue – so I had to try to do something. I eventually got the door open but it took me a while. It was one of those silly things that had a little tiny catch behind the door. There wasn't even a proper door handle on it – it was one of those things you had to put your hand in and try and pull it open – so that was what I was busy with, all I was thinking about and trying to do.

The other cars were building up behind – that was the surreal part about it, because nobody came down past. There we were in the tunnel and, as you can imagine, by this time the traffic had built up into a long queue in both lanes behind us. But for several moments nobody else moved. They just sat there.

Lisa: Yeah, but you could have gone on driving yourself, couldn't you?

Graham: (*Laughs incredulously*) Well! I *could* have done!

Lisa: So it was like, I've got to do something now, and then you did it? There was no 'shall I, shan't I'?

Graham: No, the only 'shall I, shan't I' was when I was going to push him into the wall, and then I thought about the £1,000 I'd just spent on a respray job for the truck, so I thought, 'I'm not doing that. I'll go in front and stop him.'

Lisa: I mean, you could just have thought, 'Blooming nutter. Drunk.' And driven past and gone on your way. That's what a lot of people would have thought and done.

Graham: Well . . . I suppose the police training might have had something to do with it, because obviously in every situation like that you are very curious about it. I have been in situations like this before. It was just automatic. You just go into automatic pilot.

I think the other people behind must have thought that they were witnessing a road-rage incident. They thought I was ripping his door open because I was going to knock seven bells out of him. That's what it must have looked like. They could see me trying to pull his door open and get at him inside.

Then a lady from one of the cars realised what was really happening. She came down and said, 'Is there anything I can do to help?'

I said, 'There's two young children in the car.' They hadn't made a sound. It was uncanny. They didn't cry, they didn't speak. And then another woman came down and they got the kids between them, and got them out of the car. One was about three and the other would be about five.

The driver was out of it. He had no idea what was going on, he was dead to the world. His eyes were closed. I left him where he was, just put his head forward to stop him from choking, because he was making a peculiar gurgling noise, and satisfied myself that he was still breathing.

I had no idea what was wrong. He'd had a bang on his head, probably from when he'd hit the crash barrier. You could see where he'd banged the side of his head, so it looked as though he'd knocked himself out. But how he had got himself into that position, I had no idea.

And then gradually more people started wandering down. There was a Shell tanker driver just immediately behind. He said to me, 'I've phoned the police and they are on the way.'

I said, 'Are you loaded with petrol?'

He said, 'Yes.'

I said, 'In this tunnel? Do you think it might be a good idea . . . ?'

He said, 'I'm going!'

So he cleared that lane by driving off. Another chap came down and said, 'The emergency services won't be able to get in here, because all the road is blocked with cars.'

I said, 'Can you get all the traffic moving?'

So he was there moving the traffic on, keeping one lane open all the time, until we could hear the sirens coming down. And then the police turned up. The police came down first, and the ambulance turned up shortly after them. Then the fire brigade turned up as well. I spoke to the officer in charge. I gave him my details and I said, 'Am I all right now to go?'

And he said, 'Yes, indeed.' And I just drove on my way.

Lisa: Gosh! That was such a lucky escape, wasn't it?

Graham: Yes. If he'd carried on and they'd got out of the tunnel at the far end, he could have crossed over into the other carriageway, because there are not the crash barriers down the centre after the tunnel. There could have been the most terrible crash.

Lisa: What did you think when you got back in the car?

Graham: I didn't think of anything much at first. I just drove off. It wasn't such an unusual experience for me in a way. I've always been involved with motor sports, you see. I was involved with the RAC rallies in the late seventies, and all the way through until the late 1980s; maybe even 1990 was when I did my last RAC rally. My voluntary job for years was helping with any rescue. We had a Range Rover. I used to sit there with all the bells and whistles, all the cutting equipment, and we always carried a doctor with us, so I've always been used to that sort of discipline. We've gone to cars that have been smashed up, in motor sport, and cut the drivers out. And whenever an incident had finished, we'd just leave it and go and get set up to be ready for the next one. And that's how it's always been, most of my adult life that's what I've done. Not exactly like a fireman who's doing it all the time, but enough to make it something I knew how to deal with.

It was probably about an hour afterwards, when I got to the caravan and sat down that I thought, 'Well!' So I phoned my mate up and said, 'You know, a weird thing has just happened to me.' And I related the story to him.

He just said, 'Flippin' heck!' (*Laughs*) Then it dawned on me what had happened. But it was no more and no less than what we'd been doing in the past, really. Given the situation, something had to be done.

Many years ago I'd been up to Manchester to pick up some stuff in the Range Rover. On the way back, coming along the A57 – a single carriageway, busy main road, lots of traffic – there was a group of big women at a bus stop, and it struck me as funny. They looked as though they had been playing bingo, about five or six of them, all waiting for the bus. And suddenly a set of wheels came off a wagon, big double wheels. The wheel nut had come off. Very often that does happen, wagon wheels do come off. I said to the guy with me, 'They are coming straight towards those women.' So I just edged the Range Rover forward, and intercepted the wheels, got in between the massive wagon wheels as they were running along, and the women, and they hit us and smashed into the front of the Range Rover. And the women never even realised what had happened.

Lisa: *But I mean, could it have killed them?*

Graham: Of course it could. They each weigh quarter of a ton, 500 hundredweight, and they were two fixed together.

Lisa: *And those women never even noticed?*

Graham: No, they had no idea.

Lisa: *Now if that had been me, funnily enough, I wouldn't have taken any notice either. If I was just chatting to my friends . . . But you saved their lives! Just like you saved the lives of that guy and those two children.*
  Now tell me a bit more – you phoned your friend when you got to your caravan . . . and then, did you just go straight back to work or what?

Graham: No, it was evening. I went down to the pub and chatted to people down there I knew. Told them that a rather strange thing had happened.

Lisa: *A strange thing! And what did they say, in the pub?*

Graham: They were quite amazed by the whole thing, really.

Lisa: *And what about your family? Did you tell them?*

Graham: Yeah. When I got home I did. They were quite chuffed about it.

Lisa: *But nobody found about it, did they? I mean, not publicly . . .*

Graham: No, and it wouldn't have ever been found out if a *Warrington Guardian* reporter hadn't been in our local a month later. It hit the news then because Austin, the local landlord at the pub, was telling this *Warrington Guardian* reporter that he didn't think very much of the stories they had in the local paper at the time. The reporter was actually a photographer who goes into the pub. And Austin used to be a rugby player at Warrington and he used to be quite friendly with the photographer and the people on the *Warrington Guardian*. And he was saying to this chap that there were no good stories in the paper these days, it was all rubbish, and he said, 'I'll tell you a good story.' And he related what I'd told him. And within three minutes we had the *Guardian* reporter and photographer at the house.

I was in the workshop just messing around, building something or other, and they walked in. I didn't know who they were at first. They said they wanted the whole story. So I told them what had happened – a bit reluctantly, but I did eventually tell them what had gone on.

Lisa: *So when it all came out, what happened? I mean obviously your family already knew about it and people at the pub.*

Graham: Oh yes. We had a big do at the pub then. Drinks all round. It cost me a fortune!

Lisa: We'll come back to that. First of all I want to know what happened to the people in the car.

Graham: I've no idea. I haven't a clue what happened then. The ambulance took them. The police wrote to me later when they wanted a witness statement. And that was all I heard. I did contact the police officer concerned, to ask him what had happened, or anything that he knew about it. They were very, very cagey about it. So I just left it at that. I didn't pursue it.

Lisa: You know, if that had happened to me, and if somebody had saved my life, I'd immediately ring up or go round to thank them the next day or when I was better. Especially with two children. Even if it was just myself I'd be round anyway.

Graham: You would think so, wouldn't you? The only thing I think is there was something not quite right, something peculiar about the whole situation. The police wouldn't even give me a name or tell me anything about it. I was never asked to go as a witness to court, and if there was a court case I would have been, so there must have been no court case. All I did was send a witness statement in as to what happened, and that was the last I heard about it.

Lisa: And so, you told a few friends, told your family, but it didn't hit the local newspaper until a month later and then all of a sudden . . . ?

Graham: And then on the Sunday the phone started ringing at about ten o'clock, and it was all the other papers trying to follow it up. They'd obviously picked it up off the *Warrington Guardian*, from a news agency in

Manchester, who had phoned round, and they wanted to know what the full story was.

I was a bit reluctant really, because I didn't know what the full story was with this other guy, because I hadn't heard anything. So I didn't know what his point of view was. I didn't want to embarrass anybody.

They just said, 'You can talk to us and tell us the whole story, but if you don't want to talk to us we'll just print something anyway.'

Lisa: Yes, it's always better to talk to them in the end.

Graham: It is. So at that point I got in touch with one agency, a news agency, and told them the whole story, and they put it out to all these other papers.

Apart from the local news, it was in the *Sun, Today, Daily Express, Daily Star* and *Daily Mail* . . . I think it was in most of them.

Lisa: What did you feel when you saw your face in the paper?

Graham: It was a bit embarrassing really. When you wake up to find your face on the front of the *Warrington Guardian*! (*Laughs*) And then all these other papers . . .

Lisa: I like this one – 'Hero escapes the limelight – Shy Graham Dennett has fled abroad after being swamped by the media following the Guardian's *exclusive on his heroic actions.'*

Graham: That's right. (*Laughs*) I thought, 'I'll disappear.' I said, 'I'm going on holiday!' Switched off my mobile. The TV tried to find me, but I had disappeared and nobody could find me. I went to Wales! (*Laughs*)

Lisa: What about your family?

Graham: Oh, they knew where I was. They just said, 'He's not here.' The telephone was on transfer through to my business partner, so everything was fine. He just answered the phone and whoever rang up he would say, 'I'm sorry, he's on holiday'. They'd say, 'How long is he away for?' He said, 'About six weeks.' That's where that 'shy hero' story came from.

Lisa: And so, you went off on holiday and then came back when . . .

Graham: When it had all quietened down. That was about a month later – I was incommunicado for about a month. I was around and about, you know, but I wouldn't answer the phone or answer the door. Apart from that I just went about my normal business, without anybody really knowing.

Lisa: And did you think about what had happened? Obviously when all this came out, you probably thought about it more?

Graham: Well I drive through the tunnel all the time. I've been through the tunnel twice today, this morning. And I go past the spot two or three times a week.

Lisa: How long after did you pass the spot?

Graham: Oh, after two or three days. I thought about it then, because the tyre marks were still on the grass, the marks were still on the crash barrier, the skid marks were still on the road. So yes, that brought it back to mind. And the marks were probably there for about twelve months afterwards. But I drive through there all the time and just don't ever think about it.

Lisa: Do you ever wonder about the man and the children?

Graham: No, not really. I suppose he might get a passing thought. I did wonder what had happened, but I never pursued it.

Lisa: I'm sure you must do. So then about a year went by before you heard about the award that we met at? The 1996 People of the Year Awards?

Graham: That's right. I got a phone call about a year later. I was coming down the M62, and there was a call on my mobile and I thought it was a wind-up at first, somebody having me on. I thought, 'RADAR? Who's RADAR?' It was a heck of a good day though, wasn't it?

Lisa: It was, yes. Who did you take with you?

Graham: My mother.

Lisa: And what did you think when you had to go up to get your award?

Graham: It was just numbing, wasn't it? It was a new experience. You just had to go with the flow. When your name comes up, your picture comes up on the big screen, like the Oscars, and you go up, and that was it. Dicky Bird took me up – he's used to it, isn't he?

Lisa: Do you think it has affected your life?

Graham: Not in the way that it has affected yours, no, it

hasn't. Yours was a terrible thing – mine wasn't. No, it hasn't affected me one way or the other. As I say, I'd been doing that type of thing for all those years before.

Lisa: Would you say that you were a hero?

Graham: No! It's just an automatic thing. It's just being able to think quickly enough. And having the wherewithal. If I'd been in a different vehicle I might not have been able to help so easily. I could have been in a vehicle where I couldn't see over the back. If I'd been in a small van, where I couldn't have seen anything out the back, I couldn't have done it. It was only being given the right vehicle, and knowing what to do.

Lisa: Yes, but still, so many people would think, 'I don't want to get involved.' And people do think that because they don't want to get involved with other people's problems, they don't want to have to give statements to the police . . .

Graham: The difficulty is these days . . . I noticed the other day when I was driving through Warrington, there was a little kid, probably about four or five years old, and he had fallen off his tricycle. The tricycle was on top of him, and he was right beside the main road. And he looked up and you could see in his eyes he wanted somebody to help him, but you have to be very careful what you do in that situation. If there had been somebody else in the car with me, I would definitely have stopped and gone and picked this lad up, dusted him down and seen he was all right. But if you are on your own, you can't do things like that these days. Because the next thing, somebody's accusing you of something . . .

Lisa: Yes. Isn't that sad? I mean, you come across to me like you've got a really caring nature. Do you believe in God?

Graham: I'm not a devout churchgoer, let's put it that way. Things do happen which do make me wonder. When you hear of terrible things happening to young children, it does tend to disturb your faith. It tends to put a doubt on it. Is that sense?

Lisa: Yes. But then good things happen too. I mean, you were the right man in the right place at the right time there.

Graham: Yes, I suppose so . . . yes, yes. Things do happen like that, and it does seem like a destiny when things like that happen at just the right time, so I suppose for that guy there and the kids, somebody was looking down on them all. There was somebody there at the right time and with the right equipment.

Lisa: Just a shame he didn't seem to appreciate it!

Graham: That's beside the point really. As long as the outcome was satisfactory – and as far as I was concerned the outcome *was* satisfactory. I was quite happy with that.

Lisa: It's four years on now?

Graham: 1995, yes. It will be just about four years. The kids will be seven and nine now.

Lisa: And life just went back to normal for you?

Graham: It did, yes. It got back into place, and that is fine.

Lisa's Reflections

Of all the people I've met for this book, Graham was probably the most unassuming. That newspaper headline said it all, 'Shy hero shuns the limelight'. Most people have enjoyed their fifteen minutes of fame, but Graham just thought, 'I'm going to get out of here if they get on to me!' And disappeared.

Graham was doing what he thought was the right thing at the right time. He had the skill to do it – and it was quite a Starsky and Hutch stunt he pulled off, when you think about it – but he also was willing to get into the hassle of helping someone in trouble.

His story speaks for itself really. He was quick, he was courageous, he did the right thing, and he saved at least three lives. It was when he saw the frightened little child that he said to himself, 'Dennett, you've got to do something about this. And you've got to do it now.' None of the people he saved, or any member of their family has ever thanked him. It really does make you wonder.

7

Maria Partridge
– Wheels on Fire!

Cheltenham

September 1998
Maria's is another 'car' story – but this time it was her own car bursting into flames – with her sister's two young children, one just a baby, strapped into the back seat – that was the ordeal that Maria had to contend with.

Maria is a bubbly personality, with gorgeous blue-green eyes and red-brown hair. She told me, 'I'm quite boring!' But I really liked Maria when I presented her with her award for courage at the Cheltenham Woman of the Year Dinner, organised by the Sue Ryder and Macmillan cancer charities, who give awards for achievement, business and courage.

I went to see Maria, and her husband Phil. We sat in a cafe in Cheltenham, and she told me what she'd been through.

Maria's Story

I'm nearly thirty-three, and I'm overweight. My life is quite boring! Just boring, everyday, really. Take the kids to school. We've got three that live with us and one that lives with my mum. I haven't actually worked for a while. I went to college for six months, but I gave it up because it was taking up too much of my time. I was going out at half eight in the morning, and I wasn't getting back until six o'clock at night. It was too much for me.

That morning, Philip had gone fishing with his younger brother Bob. I took the kids to school. Then my younger sister Diane and her two kids – Mark, who is ten now, and Kimberly, her little girl, who is three now – and I, we decided we would go into town shopping. Diane only lives a couple of streets away. They came round to my house and we all got in the car – a blue Montega Estate.

As we got round the corner I thought I could smell petrol. Diane said to me, 'Can we just stop off at the shop so I can get some fags?'

And I said, 'No', because I could smell petrol and I wanted to get straight back to the house so I could lift the bonnet up and see if everything was all right. Diane's house is about 500 metres away from mine. So I carried on to her house, but I'd only got about another 200 metres when I thought the heater of the car must be on, because my feet were suddenly quite hot. I tried to turn the switch and I realised that the heater wasn't on. I got to Diane's house and stopped the car, and my feet and my legs were bright red. I popped the bonnet and immediately the front of the car was engulfed in flames.

I'd just stopped, so Diane hadn't got out. But as I opened my door – because you have to lean right over and reach under the steering wheel, and because I'm a bit fat I opened my door first, so I could reach – I popped open the bonnet, and the whole thing just went, 'Whoosh!'

I had literally been driving the car while the engine was on fire without realising. You shouldn't ever open the bonnet if the car is on fire, because all the air gets in, but I hadn't realised it was on fire. It must have been the heat from the car engine that had been burning my legs.

As soon as I saw the flames I yelled at Diane to run in to the house and phone the fire brigade, and I shouted to the kids to get out, but they were too frightened to move. Diane and I are very close. She knew that I wouldn't let anything happen to her kids. She knew that I would get them out. First of all she had gone to get them out herself, and I had just yelled at her, 'I'll get them. Just phone for the fire brigade.'

It's difficult to explain – but Diane and I are so close, she trusts me, I trust her, it's the way we grew up. She said, 'Oh, my kids!'

And I said, 'I'll get them, just phone for the fire brigade.'

So she knew that I would not leave her kids whatever happened. And that's what I did. She trusted me, because she knew I would.

Kimberly was sitting behind me, behind the driver's seat. I was shouting and swearing, 'Get out, get out, get out!' Mark was nearly eight, and he had undone his seat belt and was starting to get out, but Kimberly froze. She was absolutely terrified. She was only about one and a half. I leapt out my side and I tried to yank her door open – but there was a child lock on, and the handle came off in my hand. So I had to run round the other side, undo the lock from inside, and then open the other back door. I yanked Mark out, who was nearest the door. Then I had to get in myself, undo Kimberly's seatbelt and drag her out literally by the scruff of her neck. And the fire by then was just devouring the car – the whole dashboard and the driver's seat were in flames. It must have been terrifying for the kids. It was very, very hot.

I didn't even think about being frightened of the fire myself. I just wanted Mark and Kimberly out, and I would have gone in and got them out whether I'd got burned or not. I did panic a little at first, when I popped open the bonnet and I realised the burning on my legs was from the flames and not from the heaters. Then the adrenaline gets your brain going, and once it gets going, you don't feel panic or pain. Your mind and body just click into action. Your mind tells you what to do and your body just obeys. So even if I had got burnt I wouldn't have felt it until I'd got them out.

It's just weird, because it all happened so quickly – in seconds. As Kimberly came out, the headlights began to explode. There were these colossal bangs. The headlights ended up in the next street, more than 50 metres away. Then the sunroof went. The tyres were melting and exploding under the car. It was an inferno. The whole car was totally engulfed before the firemen arrived.

Diane had shot into the house to get the fire brigade. I don't think she realised quite how bad the fire was at first. When I popped open the bonnet, flames were shooting out from inside the engine, and heating up the dashboard. When she came back out hardly a minute later she saw my whole car totally engulfed in flames, everything exploding, and I was just grabbing Kimberly out of the back.

I was swearing blue murder, so you can't put that. I was choking as well, because the smoke was bad. Once I'd got Kimberly out, I just couldn't stop choking. Kimberly kept saying 'Car!' in a shocked voice. I'd bought her a brand new potty the day before and she hadn't got to use it, and it got burnt in the back of the car. So she was quite devastated about her Winnie the Pooh potty!

And the thing that was really bothering me – I know this sounds weird – but it was my husband's car, Phil's car, and I hadn't asked him if I could borrow it. And he didn't know what had happened, and I'd have to tell him. I rang him on the mobile while we were waiting for the fire brigade, and I got really upset, because it hit me then what had happened. I was just sobbing down the phone to him, 'The car's gone!'

The thing was he was so far away – he was 28 miles away fishing – and he couldn't get back to help me because he had gone in his brother's car. If he had been in his own car – well, no, he couldn't have been in his own car because I'd taken it . . .

And then the fire brigade arrived and had to close two roads off. It took two fire engines to put it out. Then the firemen came to see if I was all right, and the shock had taken over, and I was crying.

I was sitting on Diane's doorstep, and I couldn't stop shaking. I was sitting on the steps of the house and I thought, 'My God! We were lucky.' We *were* lucky. Even the firemen said that. If we'd driven even just a little bit further down the road, the whole thing could have just engulfed us all in the flames before any of us could have got out.

But luckily enough I knew that if for some reason you could smell petrol, there had to be a serious problem. You shouldn't smell petrol. That's why I stopped almost at once. I meant to just open the bonnet, and if it had been something I could fix, we'd have gone on into town. If I couldn't deal with it, I'd have left the car at Diane's.

The fireman said I ought to go to hospital, but I said, 'No', but he called an ambulance anyway. Diane and the children came with me. Kimberly kept saying 'Car caught fire! Car caught fire!' I was given oxygen in the ambulance on the way to the hospital and checked out when I got there and they said I was OK. A bit of smoke in my lungs was all.

All the way in the ambulance I kept thinking, 'That was

close.' And I was really upset about the car, because now I wouldn't have a car to go anywhere with.

Lisa: *What happened after you got back from the hospital?*

Maria: I know this sounds weird, but I thought it was funny. It's probably my way of dealing with things. Anything's a joke to me . . . The funny thing was, after the firemen had put the fire out, in the back of the car there was all this kids' junk – because when there are kids in the car there are always toys and paper and bags – and the fireman handed me this black handbag. He said, 'There you go, darling, I've got your handbag. I'm afraid it's all I've managed to save for you.' I hadn't the heart to tell him it was our Sophy's, and there was nothing but pens in it!

My DHSS card was in the glove compartment – that had gone. I'd bought Phil a Manchester United coat – it cost me £60. And that was on the back seat of the car. It was all burned and melted. I thought, 'Oh my God! His coat!'

Phil did come home as soon as he could. He packed all his kit up and put it in the back of Bob's car, and they gave up their fishing and just came straight back home.

Philip: She was quiet. Really, really quiet. My reaction on the telephone was just to try and calm her down. Told her to forget about the car, to stop thinking the car was important. It was the people side of it that was more important. I said to my brother, 'I've got to get home.'

Maria: But you were joking about it, too, weren't you?

Philip: Well, yeah. At first. Because although she was quite hysterical to me on the phone . . .

Lisa: *(Laughs) You said, 'It's a woman!'*

Philip: Yeah. Typical woman – panicking about nothing. But when I saw the actual damage to the car the next day I was completely gobsmacked. I've seen other cars that have been on fire – but this was totally gutted. There was nothing left of it. The sunroof was gone, the tyres had melted, there was no rubber left on any of the tyres, the lights had gone. I could see how intense the heat had been.

Maria: The next day Phil and I went round to Diane's – and the car! It was a nightmare. You know how joy-riders will take a car and burn it? It was like that. Completely gutted. I just thought, 'My God, that was close!' Someone must have been looking after me that day.

Lisa: *So that night, did you keep going over and over it?*

Maria: Yes, all I could picture was Kimberly in the back of this car, and the door handle coming away in my hand. It was a good job she wasn't in the car seat, because with the car seat it's like crossing your chest, and it's complicated to undo, I might never have got her out. But she was just wearing an ordinary seat-belt.

I kept seeing two images – one was my burnt-out car, and the other was Kimberly in the back of the car. That's all I could see. I even pictured me *not* getting to her, and Kimberly dead in the back of the car. That's the worst thing I have – seeing that over and over.

I just kept thinking about it. The thing was, the car was still there for about a week before it got taken away by the insurance company. As soon as you turned the corner you could see it. And there was his ruined Manchester United coat still on the back seat of an estate car that was totally burnt out. The windscreen and the back window were completely black and cracked, absolutely charcoal.

Lisa: And when did the media learn about it?

Maria: Yes, well, talk about being on the spot – there was this bloke from the *Echo* office – the *Cheltenham Echo* – on the corner of the road just as the car caught fire. He happened to be in the right place at the right time for a story.

He came up to me as we were waiting for the fire brigade and said, 'What's happening?'

I just politely said to him, 'Go away.' In so many words.

And then the fire brigade arrived and told him to move on. Then after the fire brigade had put the fire out, while I was waiting for the ambulance he came back again, and Diane spoke to him and told him what he wanted to know.

He came back the next day to take a photograph of Kimberly, Mark and me by the car. So he got his story then. It was in the paper the following night – on the front page.

Lisa: So what did you think when you saw that?

Maria: 'Look at the state of me!' I just laughed, I thought it was so embarrassing. People didn't realise it was me until after that, so then everyone had to go and take a look at the car.

I know a lot of taxi drivers because I used to be one, and when I got in a taxi after that they'd say, 'Where's your car?'

And I'd say, 'My car's burned.'

And they'd say, 'Oh, that was you, was it? It was a right mess, wasn't it?'

People kept saying to me, 'Oh, I do think that was brave.' I'd say, 'No, it's not. Anybody would have done it.' But nobody ever believes you. Like spontaneous combustion it is – it just happened.

Lisa: That's a good word for it! Did you ever think someone was looking after you that day? I mean, do you believe in God?

Maria: Ah. I do and I don't. To me, if there was a God, there would be no starving children, so I don't know. When your number's up, your number's up. Mine wasn't due that day. It's just that – you know what you want to say, but you just can't explain it. I can't find the words.

Lisa: So it was just in the local paper that evening and that was it?

Maria: Until I got the award. And that was funny. Do you want the truth or not? It was the following February, about half past six at night and the doorbell rang. I looked through the spyhole and I saw this posh-looking lady and I thought, 'Oh dear, I haven't got any money this week.' I thought it was the club lady, coming round for her catalogue money, so I nearly didn't answer it. But then I opened the door and I said, 'Hello?'
    And she said, 'Mrs Partridge?'
    And I thought, 'Do I say yes or do I say no?'
    But I said, 'Yeah?'
    She said, 'Oh I'm from the Sue Ryder Home, la, la, la' – ever so posh! And then she turned round and said, 'We would like to present you with this letter. Don't read it now. Read it when I've gone and ring me back.'
    There was this big plastic envelope and I thought, 'Oh, no.' So I looked in it and her name was Gillian Rose. I didn't know who she was from Adam. So I read this letter

and it said I'd been nominated for the Woman of the Year Award for courage. Blah blah blah. And I actually thought somebody was taking the mick. So I thought, yeah, right. Basically it said that I'd won the award, and the ceremony would be at the Pump Rooms – big posh place. I don't often go there, anyway.

I read it again and I thought, 'Never!'

So I was quite excited, but I was embarrassed as well. Then Phil's brother phoned. I said, 'You'll never guess what!'

He said, 'What is it?' I read him the letter. He said, 'A hero!'

And then a couple of days later Gillian rang me again. She said, 'If you accept this you're going to have it presented by Lisa Potts.' And I thought that was an honour in itself. I know you think I'm jesting, but you ask Phil. What happened at that school, I thought you were a real hero. So I was chuffed that I was going to meet you.

But then it was like – we don't have a lot of money. I was wondering what I was going to wear, where we were going to get the money from, but then my sister bought me an outfit. And Phil bought me something as well. Phil bought me a shirt, didn't you? And Diane bought me a suit.

Lisa: *A silver one. I've got the photograph at home. You looked lovely. You're both on it. You looked very handsome, too, in that suit.*

Maria: Oh he didn't! He's a poser anyway!

Philip: Gillian Rose got it for me.

Maria: Gillian Rose had him fitted for that suit because she knew we couldn't afford it. She said it was my day and they were going to spoil me. Even his shoes came from this place, didn't they? This bloke came to our house and fitted him out, and they paid for it all.

Philip: They really looked after us. They were nice. I won the Lord Lindley rug in the raffle, the Lord Lindley throw. I've still got it. It's in the box.

Lisa: Did it feel nice that somebody had remembered?

Maria: It did actually, it was nice. But I was more worried by that day than I was the day the car caught fire. Because for me going to the Pump Rooms for a dinner – it was £45 a ticket – because I'm not used to it, and it was very official and I've never been to an official thing in my life. And then when the tickets come through the post, and they were £45 each and I just thought, 'I can't pay that!' But it was free for us. My mate Shirley did my hair for me.

Lisa: That night when I met you I thought you were pretty calm both of you.

Maria: I wasn't, I was terrified.

Lisa: Were you? I was just worried that I looked fat in my dress . . .

Maria: I looked fat in my trousers. When we got there he was going for the champagne. I don't like champagne and I was taking a sip of it, being polite, and I thought, 'This is horrible!' But he drank his and the – what do you call them, the person that bangs the floor to say dinner's ready? I can't think of the word – oh, the toastmaster. She banged the floor and said, 'Could you take your seats.' He ran back and got more champagne!

Philip: Why not? Chance of a lifetime, isn't it?

Lisa: Who did you sit at a table with?

Maria: People I didn't know. And they kept saying, 'Oh, you were very brave! Blah, blah, blah.' And all this lot. And we were sitting round the table woman, man, woman, man, so we weren't next to each other – and this bloke next to me bought a bottle of wine. And all I could keep thinking was, 'Oh my life, I hope we have enough money to buy one.' We only had £20 between us. I thought it was going to be everyone taking it in turns to buy the wine. I thought, 'I hope and pray that he has enough money to buy a bottle.' But we didn't have to.

And then, there were little envelopes on the table. And I thought, 'What's this?' It was £5 to go on a raffle and I'm thinking, 'Oh, never!' And this lady near me, she had some money donated to her, and she said, 'I'd like you to put your name on one envelope, and I'd like your husband to put his name on another envelope.' And of course, when he won this rug they were all going, 'Oh bravo! Well done!' You know? And then he had to go up and get it. All these people were coming up and going, 'Oh, you are lucky. I'd like to have won that. I wanted to win that!' Even you, Lisa, came up and said, 'I'd like to have won that!'

And then when they were giving the awards, and I wasn't first, was I? I was in the middle. And when you called my name out, my legs went to jelly. And I thought, 'Don't give up on me, legs!'

I got my award from you, and I got back to the table and he was taking a photograph, and he had a tear in his eye, and I looked at him and I don't know why I said it, but I said, 'You sap!'

Yes, I got back to the table and he was crying. I said, 'You sap!'

And there were these free samples on the table, like perfume, and I kept shoving them all in my handbag. And there were sweets and they told me to take some home for my kids. He had pockets full. And then they were clearing up and going to take the flower decorations out, and my sister-in-law, Mandy – you must put this bit in, because she'll kill me – she said to me, 'I want a table decoration.' So I took the one off my table. And then there was one on a table on its own, and this lady said to me, 'You can have that one if you want to.' So I picked it up, too.

Then this other lady came up to me and she went, 'Excuse me, I think that is mine.'

So I said, 'Oh, but she said I could have it.'

Then she turned round and said, 'Oh I do beg your pardon. Yes, of course you can have it. Please accept my apologies and take it.'

Lisa: That was really because you were the VIP – nobody was going to mess with you that night!

Maria: Yes! When we got home we were laughing, weren't we? We were offered a lift home. But the thing is, where we live, it's like a crummy estate, right? If you leave a decent car there for two minutes, they have the wheels off. This man comes up and says to me, 'How are you?' And he talked really posh, and he said, 'Would you like a lift home?'

I thought, 'There's no way!' So I said, 'His brother's coming to pick us up.'

He said, 'I would have been delighted to take you.'

Where we were, if he'd have parked his car, they'd have had the wheels off before he'd taken it out of gear.

Lisa: Never mind, he could probably afford a new car! But when you were receiving all that, did you think about why?

Maria: I did. To be honest, I thought it was a lot of fuss about nothing. It was just something that happened, that I would have done no matter where I was, no matter who it was. If I'd seen it happen to a car across the other side of the street, and I didn't know who was in it, I would have done exactly the same thing.

I remember standing on my doorstep having my photograph taken. And this bloke over the road said, 'Cor, you've scrubbed up well, haven't you?'

The next evening there was a tiny little bit about it again in the paper, with a photograph – 'Woman exhausted on the steps'!

Lisa: Has the whole experience had any lasting ill effects on you? Or on Kimberly?

Maria: On Kimberly, I'd say it did. She doesn't like going in cars now. When we got another car, she wouldn't get in it, she said, 'No catch fire. No catch fire.'

I said, 'No, this one won't, love.'

And even now, when we go out in the car, Phil gets his hair off at me sometimes, because if I can smell petrol, I slip my seat-belt off and my hand is on the door ready to get out. He says, 'There isn't anything.'

I say, 'There is.'

He says, 'There *isn't!*'

Any time I smell petrol it reminds me of that day and I think, 'This car could blow up again.' Because that's the second car fire I've been in. The first one was a little tiddly one. That was a big one. If three strikes, you're out. I could get caught in another car fire and I could be a gonner. Everything happens in threes to me.

Lisa: *I hope not! (Laughs)*

Philip: We just don't seem to have any luck . . .

Maria: No, there's no luck in our lives . . .

Lisa: But you're happy? I mean, I always think, with things I get that go wrong, 'God, I'm so lucky to be here.' And I have to remember that. It's taken me three years to be able to sit where I'm sitting now. I'd have had to sit where you are sitting, with my back to the wall, and facing the door – and I still have to force myself to sit with my back to people. It's taken that long to say to myself, 'Now don't be stupid.' But it is psychological. Loads of things. I do mad things. Like you know when you get in a lift? And people get in with you? I feel I've got to get out of the lift. I have to say to myself, 'No, you can't.' Otherwise you spend your whole life running away.

You say you've got no luck, but there are people in the world with masses and masses of money and they often seem far less happy than you two. I've spent time with lots of these people . . . I've seen that. You are rich with something else.

Maria: I know they say you can't buy happiness with money, but if I won the lottery – I wouldn't like to win millions and millions – I'd just like to win enough to take me and my kids on holiday. Because they have never, ever been on holiday. But me, with my luck, if I find a ten pound note, it would probably be a forgery. And I'd get arrested trying to spend it.

But, OK. Money can't buy happiness. We've been married for how long? Fourteen years, is it? We met when

I was sixteen. I've been with him half my life, really. We're happy as we are, aren't we?

Philip: We are. If I can give our kids a sense of purpose in life, that's enough for me. That's what it's all about.

Maria: Yes, fair enough. But I don't really mean . . . if I say luck, I mean if I put a pound on a horse, it will probably fall at the first fence. That's what I mean. I'm not a lucky person at gambling. But of course, yes, I know I am lucky to be alive. And now we just have to get on with it.

Lisa's Reflections
I personally think Maria is pretty amazing. Not just for what happened that day, but for all the ways she deals with the problems in her life. And she still smiles at the end of it!

I know what she means about the adrenaline stopping you from panicking or feeling pain. She just knew she had to get the children out, no matter what, and didn't think about getting burnt herself. Just as I knew I had been attacked but I didn't know that he'd hurt me, because I needed to get those kids away as quickly as I could. A couple of bumps and scratches is nothing compared with their whole life – I mean, at one and a half, how much life had Kimberly had?

And when she grabbed Kimberly by the scruff of the neck – I remember with my children, shoving and pushing and lifting them like they were rag dolls. 'Yes, in, in, in. Get the next one in.'

Some people have a really strong character, and Maria is one. She just gets on with things. Some people react and some people don't when they see trouble ahead.

She didn't have a lot of media attention compared with some of the people, and I think she deserved more, really.

Except she probably wouldn't have wanted it. She more or less told the journalist to get lost when he first came up to her!

She was the Cheltenham Woman of the Year – which made her so nervous. It reminded me of my first award in Birmingham, when I was Midlander of the Year. I remember being equally scared, and my legs going to jelly. And then when I went up, I had won the overall award, because there were about fifteen of us, and we all won a gold pin, and then somebody wins the overall award. And when they said it was me, I couldn't get off my chair. It was absolutely awful. And when they said, 'And here to present the award are the children you saved,' I just couldn't stop crying. It was worse than the day. Whenever I see their little faces with the scars, I know I'd give every single thing back for it never to have happened.

8

Graham Roberts
– The Reluctant Hero

MoD Water Police, Portsmouth Harbour

1 April 1996

Graham got the People of the Year Award in 1996, the same year as me, so that's where I met this lovely, big Father Christmas of a man.

Graham was in the process of rescuing some children in trouble in their boat, and in doing so he fell into the water himself – by accident. But witnesses thought he'd dived in on purpose to save the children – and from then on the media called him a hero.

When I wrote to him to ask him about being in my book, Graham said, 'I'd love to see you again, Lisa, but I really don't think you should do my story. It was the most embarrassing thing ever – all those awards, being on the television, in the newspapers. Do come and see me, but please don't interview me. Please don't put me in your book!' Despite his protests, I'm still going to include

Graham's story, because it tells you a lot about how the media goes about making someone into a hero for a day.

Graham's Story

My name is Graham James Roberts if you want the full works. I'm forty-nine years old. I'm a constable in the Ministry of Defence Police. I've been in the job for twenty-two years this October. I live in Gosport, in Portsmouth Harbour. I've got my own semi-detached house where I live with my wife and two daughters, a mortgage and a car! All the usual.

I'm six foot tall, grey hair with a grey beard, which I've had for the best part of eighteen years. I weigh about 17 stone. I've been called both Father Christmas and Kenny Rogers!

At the time of the incident, I was employed as a constable coxswain in the Ministry of Defence Police Marine Unit, a marine policing unit which operates out of Portsmouth Naval Base. Ministry of Defence Police is a civilian force – we're not anything to do with the military, although we work for the Ministry of Defence.

I did that job for nearly seven years, until two years ago. I'm still in the Ministry of Defence police, but I've left the Marine Unit. I'm now at a defence munitions depot in Gosport, which is the old Royal Naval Armament Depot. So I look after badgers and foxes and make sure nobody gets into the place.

The MoD Marine Unit normally have two launches that patrol Portsmouth Harbour and the Solent. And they enforce all the regulations for the Queen's Harbourmaster, because Portsmouth is a dockyard port, controlled by the Queen's Harbourmaster, for all the warships coming in and out of harbour. It's a pretty busy water unit. Portsmouth is quite a big harbour, and then you've got the Solent, where all the shipping goes up to Southampton as well, so we get quite a few incidents involving ferries, warships, yachts, jet-skis and of course merchantmen as well.

You're responsible for everything – enforcing the speed limits, security of the naval base, Ministry of Defence establishments that back end onto the harbour. So there's security of everything involved. I should say there are probably ten thousand yachts in Portsmouth Harbour – I hope that's not too big an exaggeration. Say between eight and ten thousand that are actually moored. There's a terrific amount of theft that goes on from the vessels. So it's not just attending incidents with boats.

It's like all police work; some days you can have three or four incidents in an hour, and another day you can have nothing happen at all. Portsmouth Water is quite a busy place, so you get quite a few minor incidents. Normal policing can be a very depressing job, but our job on the water was good, because 95 per cent of your work was helping people. Even if it's just a small boat that's broken down in the middle of the harbour with a sixty-seven thousand pound ferry bearing down on it – you nip out, drop a quick line to them and tow them out of the way. Two minutes' work and that's somebody who is saved from quite a lot of difficulty. It gives you a real buzz.

It's not like vehicles. Most people have got a driving licence for their vehicles. On the water, anybody can get into a boat and set off, so you get people with all sorts of problems. I had an Assistant Chief Constable's Commendation for a job that we did earlier in the same year. That was when HMS *Illustrious* was coming into harbour, and a yacht had disabled itself, damaged its rudder by hitting one of the forts. He had a wife and two thirteen-year-old girls on board and he was deaf. He was down below trying to use the radio to call assistance, and the *Illustrious* was coming into harbour, and this yacht went right across the front. We tried everything to get it to turn out of the way. There was no way that the wife could steer it. She was hysterical, the girls were hysterical and in the end the yacht went one way, I went astern, and the bows of the *Illustrious*, which is one of the largest carriers, came straight down through the middle of us. I nipped round the back of the carrier, and as it came round the other side I could see they were clear. But their mast hit one of the sponsons, which is a bit that sticks out, and was knocked down. So we had to help them off their boat and take them in. They were so relieved and pleased to be safe on board. And you went home at the end of the day and thought, 'That did a bit of good.' That's the part of the job I really miss now I'm not doing it any more.

People like the water – they like to play on it. In the summer you get a lot of pleasure craft incidents. We've had small dinghies rowing across Portsmouth Harbour with as many as six people in them, and just about an inch from the top of the boat to the water. You just have to pull them out of the water and say, 'Please. One or two people maybe, but not six.' You get swimmers, children, dogs, all sorts using the water.

You go to anything that the Southern Coastguard call you to. There's the Gosport and Fareham Inshore Rescue service that operates from Stokes Bay. They are all volunteers. Our police launches are on the water twenty-four hours a day, so they usually attend anything that happens. Fires on boats. Boats sinking, so you have to get the family off and try and tow their boat back to shore somehow.

The people whose boat is sinking are very grateful to be able to get on a launch that is floating. I've had some lovely letters from people. You don't think of it as an amazing job at the time, but they think you've done something wonderful because they are mainly amateurs. That's not to be derogatory. They do it for pleasure. But they tend to forget things like the fact that water gets shallow in places. We've seen boats lose their propellers and their engines and sink within minutes because they've gone over shallow water and broken up. And you get walkers stuck on the mudflats in Portsmouth because the tide's gone out, and left them stranded.

We work with the Southern Coastguard helicopter as well. They exercise with us in Portsmouth. We work closely with it, in searches for people in distress – people who have fallen overboard from ferries and private yachts and gone missing. In the years that I was on the boat we had quite a few people drowning in Portsmouth Harbour, and that's always very sad. But on the whole, it was the most rewarding work I've ever done.

I can't possibly forget the date of the incident you want me to talk about, because it was 1 April, All Fools' Day, 1996. It was very apt, believe me. And I'm pretty sure it was a Monday.

We were due to start at two o'clock, and normally we used to get in at about half past one, quarter to two. We had literally just arrived and were taking over duty from the crew that was going off, when we got a radio message from the control room that there were three boys in difficulty, trapped between the submarines moored in Porchester Creek. That is probably not more than a mile away from our base unit, which is at the top, by the Continental Ferry Board at Portsmouth Harbour. We knew where the submarines were moored, because of course when you patrol the harbour the whole time you know exactly where everything – or most things – are.

There were three of us on board: Sergeant Chris Simon; another constable coxswain, Dave Masters; and myself. They always have a crew of three – a sergeant and two PCs, all qualified coxswains in accordance with Royal Yachting Association standards. So we shot off at top speed to Porchester Creek, straight away as soon as we got the message. We were in Police Launch 7303 – a fast motor-launch, which is capable of about 25 to 28 knots when it is new. It had just been overhauled, so we were there in no time.

All we knew was that there were some youngsters in difficulty trapped between the submarines. That was the message we got from the Southern Coastguard. A yachts-man had reported seeing them. He actually found them by chance as he was leaving the harbour. He heard them calling for help, and had passed the message to Southern Coastguard, who contacted us, so all we knew was that there were some youngsters in difficulties, in a dinghy between the submarines.

It was a grey, cloudy day. It wasn't raining. There was a good force-four breeze I would say, a strong breeze, and the tide was flowing quite rapidly so there was a little bit of choppy water. The three little boys were in a small fibreglass dinghy. We had to slow right down as we arrived, because the wash that the boat makes can create quite a disturbance for a small dinghy.

Once we arrived at the bow of the submarines, which was about 50 feet away from where they were, down between the subs, we could see what the situation was. They must have drifted down with the wind and tide between the subs, but they hadn't the strength to row back out again. There were three young lads in the dinghy, and one of them was standing up screaming at the top of his voice. Two of them were sitting and crying, they weren't able to do anything at all. They only looked like seven- or eight-year-olds, but in fact they were nine and eleven, I believe. But they were very frightened and at the end of their tether.

The bows of the two submarines were moored to each other by cable, which is very thick steel cable, like a ten-inch chain. The two submarines were held together by lines. The lines allow them room to spring apart and come together in the water. The boys were at the far end, between them like the filling in a sandwich, and it was like looking down a long tunnel at them. What the boys were holding on to was one of the ropes, called a spring rope, that goes from the front of one submarine to midships of the other submarine. And the oldest lad was standing, holding onto it with his hands up over his head. He's holding onto the rope with his hands, and his feet are holding the dinghy in position against the tide and the wind. He was screaming his head off for help. The other two weren't able to do anything. And this young lad that was holding onto the rope, was clinging on like mad, because the tide was trying to drag the dinghy further down in between the two submarines, where they were resting together. The wind and tide were too strong for them to be able to row out. They'd just got tired out.

We could get to the bow end, but to get to them we would have to take the boat in underneath the thick steel cable. We might have knocked the mast off the boat, because we had a small mast, but it was the only way to get to them quickly. If there had been more time, and if we had been sure the lad was able to hold on, we could have put our boat alongside the submarine, gone up onto the submarine, and got a line down to them and then taken them forward.

Now the trouble with submarines, they are not like ordinary ships where they've got straight sides. They are like rounded tanks. We were very concerned that he was going to let go – and he was screaming that he couldn't hold on any longer. I thought, 'If we don't get a line to him very quickly, that boat is going to turn', because the tide was rushing quite fast now between the submarines, and because the sides are rounded, it could have flipped their boat over on its side.

It's extremely dangerous between those submarine hulls – they drift apart, but the vessels are 250 feet in length. They weigh about – I'm guessing now, I should know because I'm an ex-navy man – if I said 2,000 to 2,500 tons I'm not too far wrong. A frigate weighs about 2,700 tons. Now if you imagine, they float apart, and then they drift together. There's nothing to hold them. No man could hold them apart. So if they had drifted together – they would have been crushed. Arms, legs, heads. It doesn't bear thinking about, really.

And if their boat had flipped over, once they were in the water, I was convinced they would have gone down. Again, because of the shape of a submarine, and the fact that they were tied together, you had what was like an undertow, because the water was rushing in and then being forced down under the submarines. So had they gone in, the three of them would almost certainly have been pulled underneath the submarines and drowned before we could get to them.

So we had to get a line to them as quickly as possible. To do that, we had to take the bow of our police launch under the cable. It was a bit of a risk to our boat, but that didn't matter. I positioned myself right in the bow, ready to throw them a line.

I'd made my life-jacket up on the way. It's like a combined jacket that you are issued with, a sea-safe jacket. I did the zip up and buttons up, and it has got an automatic life-jacket in it. We'd all done that on the way there, because you do. We still couldn't really get that close, so I put two lines together to make a line long enough to reach them. The head rope and the stern rope together would have been long enough to reach their boat, so I knotted the two together. Quite easy to do – quick bowline and they are perfectly joined. They are safe. As any mariner will tell you, they'd trust their life on a bowline.

So I had the line ready in the bow. The helmsman was on the wheel, and Chris was on the port side a little bit further back from me.

I'm shouting to the lads as we went in under the cable, 'Just hold on.' I really needed him to hold on just long enough for us to get a line to them. I said, 'We'll be with you in a second. Just hold on and we'll get a rope to you.'

He was screaming, 'I can't hold on any longer!' He sounded really desperate.

I have the rope coiled in my hand, my legs braced on a rail at the front of the boat. And as soon as I thought I could reach him, I threw the line. I was confident that I could reach them, but I had to use a full arm action and throw the coil rope quite forcefully.

At the exact moment that I threw the line, our boat hit the side of the submarine and literally stopped dead, bang – and I went straight off head first into the water. The forward momentum, as well as my being off balance because of throwing the rope, just took me overboard. It's like in a car, if it stops suddenly you get thrown forward. Well that's what happened. The boat stopped and the next thing I knew I was in the water.

The bow of our launch is about 3 feet above the water, which isn't very far, really, but in the second that it took me to fall from the bow into the water I thought, 'This is going to be cold!' Your head goes first into the water, and everything's green and grey, because unfortunately Portsmouth Harbour is not like being in the tropics. Visibility is about 3 feet, when it's good! It was all going greyer and darker as I was going down, and I was thinking, 'I wish I hadn't done that.' And then my life-jacket started automatically inflating, and your mind quickly thinks, 'Oh, that's good, the life-jacket is working. And I bobbed back up to the surface. I still had the other end of the rope in my hand.

That was the really silly thing. I threw them one end, which went straight into their boat, perfectly, and I took the other end into the water with me. You've got to smile about it, Lisa. I even did at the time. Afterwards I thought, 'If you ever want to make a fool of yourself that's the way to do it. Throw someone one end of the line, and then fall in the water with the other end.' I mean I'm an ex-sailor, I should have known to make the other end secure on the launch before I threw it. I did twelve years in the navy. I should have known better.

But it all happened so quickly. You really do just want to get to them quickly when they are so young. Because they are small. Because they are frightened and vulnerable. All I could think of was getting this young lad a line, because he was really screaming. They must have been there for some time even before the yachtsman saw them. They couldn't row out, because the tide was pushing them back in.

Lisa: Did you think you were risking your own life?

Graham: No, no. Not at all. I was with a police launch. I was used to being on the water. Even when I was in the water, I had safety equipment on. I was wearing a good life-jacket.

It was still cold! That was one of the things that surprised me afterwards, how quickly the cold water takes all your strength away.

But to get back to where I threw them the rope. It was a lovely throw! Right into their boat. When I came up, I bobbed up like a cork. Then I swam straight over to the children. The tide took me there naturally, anyway, and by this time I was only 20, 30 feet away from them.

People said to me afterwards that I could have tried to get myself out of the water, but we were there for the kids, and they were terribly frightened. They looked ever so small and vulnerable, between the submarines. So I swam over to the dinghy, and the lad was having trouble with the line he was holding on to because it was quite high for him. But I managed to kick myself up out of the water, grab the line and pulled it right down for him, which meant that he could then put his arms over the top of it, so he could hold on a bit better. So I was in the water, at the back of the dinghy, just holding on and steadying them, and I said to the lads, 'Just sit still, keep calm, and we'll get another line to you in a few seconds.'

Lisa: What were the other guys in the police boat doing at this point?

Graham: Well, Chris was a bit concerned, because he now had four people to worry about, three boys in the dinghy, and a man in the water. But they were in the right position now, the boat was under the wire, and they could get another line across to the boys.

It's very, very indistinct now, what happened after that. I was in the water holding onto the dinghy, and another line came across. I couldn't tell you whether Chris or Dave threw it. But we had their boat steady then. We had them under our control.

Lisa: And what were the little boys doing?

Graham: Oh! Still crying! They were all very, very frightened and distressed. The young lad in the television interview, when it was re-enacted for the BBC's *999 Lifesavers*, said he thought I was very, very brave. But that was because he thought I'd dived in on purpose, to save them when, in fact, it was the last thing I should have done. I'd created an extra problem for the others on the launch.

What happened then was the police launch dropped the second line to the dinghy, I swam along at the back, pushing the dinghy and just making sure it was steady and didn't tip over when it was being pulled along. Then the police launch turned astern and pulled them out very slowly with their powerful engine. And so I was towed out as well, really. I was being rescued as well as the boys. And that's the truth of the matter.

The last thing you want to do in a rescue situation, when you are trying to get someone out of a dangerous situation, is to go in the water yourself. I mean, there are times when you might have to, when there is no other way. But it's absolutely the last thing you do, because you then become part of the incident. The plan was just to throw them a line as quickly as possible, and we could have towed them straight out, and it would have been five minutes and they'd have been OK.

Lisa: *It's very quick, the whole thing, isn't it? But I mean, you could have tried to get back in the police boat, but you didn't, you swam out to help the boys.*

Graham: There was no real thought to it. The kids were there, frightened, and that's what we were there for. I was in the water – the tide was taking me towards them, the wind was taking me, which is how they had got there themselves. I could stick with them and help keep them calm and steady. There was nothing else I could do that was useful. When I got up to them I was able to think, 'We're all right now. There's time.'

It must have looked to the yachtsman – who had

reported the incident and was watching the whole thing
– as well as to the boys as though I'd dived in on purpose;
and that was the dreadful thing, because I didn't. It was
purely an accident. It was completely the wrong thing to
do, and could have made matters much worse if I'd got
into trouble myself.

The best moment was when I saw the boys being lifted
from the dinghy onto the police boat and knew they were
going to be all right. That was a great feeling of relief.
None of them had fallen in the water.

I thought, 'That's fine . . . Now, how are you going to
get yourself out?' Like an idiot, you know. Getting the
boys out was really good, that was the thrill. I remember
thinking, if nothing else goes right, at least they are out of
danger and everything's OK.

In the end I had to be hauled out myself. There was no
way I could get back up onto our boat, 3 feet above the
waterline, even with the other two men hauling me. I
must have weighed all of 20 stone with all that water in
my clothes. They tried, but it was impossible. So I had to
swim across maybe 15, 20 feet to the Hampshire Police
launch, which by then was standing by and had a landing
platform at the back I could climb up on, and from there
into their launch.

The whole episode had only taken ten minutes, but
even in that time the cold gets to you very, very quickly.
Once the boys were all safely on the MoD launch, I was
pulled out of the water by the Hampshire Police – rescued
if you like – they took me back to our base. I said to them,
'What an idiot!' They work on the water the same as
ourselves. They know the rules.

I had been having trouble breathing because the life-
jacket had come up around my neck. It inflates, and it had
tightened round my neck, so I was having a little bit of
difficulty breathing once I got out of the water. I hadn't

noticed while I was in the water. They got me back to the naval base as quickly as possible and there was an ambulance waiting there, because I was shivering quite a lot.

I'd also damaged my leg, because where I had been holding the rail between my knees, when I went off the boat, it drove a bolt into my shin, which I didn't realise until I was in the ambulance. I hadn't realised at all while I was in the water – because of the cold and the shock, I suppose.

While I was in the ambulance the crew undressed me, and wrapped me in a blanket – that's when I realised I had hurt my leg. I had an egg on my shin, the size of a goose-egg. I couldn't believe it. It left a nice hole. It took about six weeks to heal.

So I was taken up to Queen Alexandra Hospital. I spent about an hour and a half there. They checked me for hypothermia. Hypothermia, as you probably know, is when your core temperature gets really low. As you get cold your body withdraws all the heat into the vital organs, so that's why your muscles get weak, because they don't get the blood supply. But I was fine, I wasn't hypothermic at all. I was just very cold, but my inner temperature was fine. Then they X-rayed my leg, but there was no break or anything, so it was just the puncture. So I was fine, and I had to get back to base. Someone brought up some dry clothes for me, to the hospital, so I could get dressed. The press were at the hospital trying to speak to me before I was even dry. That amazed me. The nurse came in and said, 'There's some press outside would like to speak to you.'

I said, 'I'm terribly sorry, I can't.' Because of my job, we're not allowed to speak to the press direct. I told them to go to the public relations office at the naval base. I felt dreadful, because falling off the boat was such a mistake. I was very embarrassed about the whole thing. I mean, I'm an experienced seaman. I joined the navy as a boy seaman, served for twelve years, finished up as petty officer midshipman. I'd been on the police launch for the best part of six years, I'm used to dealing with small boats, and I know the rules. But just because of the circumstances and feeling we had to get a line to them quickly – I made a mistake. He was screaming so hard, this young lad. And of course, it all went wrong. But I remember being in hospital thinking, 'Oh God, the press have got hold of it already.'

Then I went back to work, because I was fine. I had to give an initial report to my bosses about what had happened, and that I was OK. They let me go home early after I'd reported in.

So I got home at five, instead of my normal time of ten, and my wife didn't know anything about it until I arrived at the door with all my clothes in a bag and said, 'Wash these, please!'

She wasn't worried about it. It's all just part of the job. I've been in the water at other incidents, but always intentionally before. You're always getting wet somehow. But once she heard the story she wasn't too impressed. But what surprised me was that my mother-in-law then telephoned to say she had heard all about it already – on Classic FM, the radio station. It had said I was in hospital suffering from hypothermia. It wasn't true, of course. I was fine. They had got my name and everything. Later Henry Kelly even sent me a bottle of champagne from the station, which was really kind.

But I felt dreadful. I was really pleased that the boys were OK, but I felt dreadful about what had happened. They had got the boys back to the base, and then their parents were called in to pick them up. They were told off good and proper by their parents. There was a lovely bit on the *999 Lifesavers* programme, with one of the boys' mums. She says, 'I told him off in the police station, I told him off outside, I told him off all the way home in the car, I told him off when we got indoors, I told him off when he went upstairs to bed . . .' Then the picture cuts to him, and he says, 'She weren't very happy!' I got lovely cards from all three of them, saying thank you.

My overriding feeling was embarrassment. I shouldn't have fallen off like that. And when I knew the press were involved I was not very happy. I thought, 'Oh dear! This has all gone wrong.'

I had a reasonably quiet night. But the next day the telephone calls started.

Lisa: What were you thinking all that night?

Graham: It wasn't just that night. For the first couple of weeks I kept waking up from dreaming – and it was always the bit where I went off the boat and I'd wake up one second before I hit the water. But it wasn't horrific, and I wouldn't call it a nightmare, it was just dreaming about the incident. I can still recall that moment I went off the boat even now.

Lisa: Was it like having a 'flashback'? I have flashbacks, and I see all the dreadful things that happened. And sometimes I see myself running for the children. Is it like that, a kind of re-enactment in your mind very quickly?

Graham: It just comes back. Especially being back out on the boat and seeing the submarines in the harbour for quite some time afterwards. They've gone now. They were waiting to be scrapped. They were just two derelict vessels waiting to be taken away for scrap.

The next day I was off work, because the leg came up

very badly bruised. As the egg went down the bruising came out, and I couldn't put any weight on it for several days. So I was off for about six days, and then I went back to work with my leg bandaged. And I was fine.

But the next day the press kept telephoning. I don't know how they got my number. But there's electoral rolls, aren't there? I lived in Gosport, they obviously knew. My wife and my daughters were the barrier. My wife's an administration officer in the Ministry of Defence. She works as a contracts officer, so she's more used to that sort of thing. But I just didn't answer the telephone. There were ridiculous offers. It was stupid. But I never spoke to anyone from the press.

It doesn't make any difference. The local *Portsmouth and Gosport Evening News* got hold of it. The *Southampton Evening News*. The national dailies. Television asked me to do an interview. The *Daily Star* had it in a full spread – that was so embarrassing. I mean that was a full double-page spread – I've still got it somewhere – 'Tug-boat Hero PC Rescues Three Boys'. It was just blown up out of all proportion in the papers. Then they gave me a Gold Star Award.

Even the citation in the RADAR People of the Year Award makes me cringe every time I read it. I'd have been far happier if we'd have just got the line to the boys – they'd have held on, we'd have got them out, and that would have been the end of the matter. It's the ironic thing – if I hadn't made a mistake and fallen in the water, nobody would have heard anything about it. We'd done countless rescues without all of this.

I wanted none of it. When I was told I had been nominated for the People of the Year Award there was a terrific amount of pressure on me from senior officers to accept it, because of the good publicity for the MoD. But in all honesty the only reason I did accept it in the end was because they told me Dicky Bird was going to be there! And he was. I think he's a really great character.

But the nice thing was a lot of old friends contacted me as well. It made the front page of the London *Evening Standard*.

Lisa: *How did your wife and daughters feel? Are they proud of you?*

Graham: Well they are. And that's the other thing that's annoying, because I've said to them, 'Well! Here you are, you're proud – and I just feel a fool.'

I also got the Chief Constable's Commendation for what I'd done. They gave it to me on the HMS *Victory*, which was very pleasing to me because I love that ship. Being an ex-naval man, I think HMS *Victory* is probably the nicest attraction that this country has. Certainly the best maritime attraction.

Lisa: *Were people recognising you in the street?*

Graham: Oh yeah, that's the truth. In the pubs afterwards, my local, different people. I was stopped down town. Even in the bank. The BBC came down and spoke to me about doing the reconstruction for *999 Lifesavers* – which they did. I agreed to do it only if they would show it as it really happened. In other words – if I threw the rope and then fell in the water. And they did actually film it quite well. Like it was.

That took three days to film and that was quite fun. I was a bit disappointed though – I wasn't allowed to fall off the boat again myself. They got someone else to do that part. But I did the interview.

People would say, 'Oh, you were on the television. I saw you.'

Lisa: How did you feel about seeing yourself on TV?

Graham: Well, that was a bit of fun because once you do see yourself on television, you've got to smile about it. It's like listening to yourself on tape. I sound completely different to myself, when I hear myself on tape. As we all do, I think. And when you see yourself on television you think, 'God, do I look like that?'

My two brothers and three sisters are all in Australia, and all my nephews and nieces are out there. So of course we sent the video of the programme out to them. So I had a lot of fun with it that way. But again, I told them the true story; the truth is, I fell off the boat.

If I hadn't fallen in the water, that incident would never have made it into the news. It might have made a little bit on the bottom of the local *Evening News* – three boys rescued by the Ministry of Defence police launch. So that's what makes me feel bad. It's true, Lisa, it's true. Even now. I was in the pub the other day, just a couple of weeks ago, and they had just rerun the BBC *Lifesavers* piece – it must have been on one of the new channels that are coming out. There's the landlord of the pub coming round the corner and saying, 'I've just seen you on the TV!'

I thought, 'Oh, no, not again.'

And people do pull your leg, don't they? 'How's the hero?' and all that.

Lisa: Do you have a faith?

Graham: Oh yes, I believe in God, that's for sure. I'm not a churchgoing man on a regular basis, but that's because of my job. I don't go every Sunday, because I can't go every Sunday. But I believe in God. And I love Christmas.

Lisa: Looking back now – do you see yourself as a different person? Has it affected you emotionally at all?

Graham: Not really. What affected me, probably, was the fuss afterwards. I would have been fine about the incident. Coming to terms with it, saying to yourself, 'Yeah. You're an idiot.' I could have coped with that. What made it more difficult to cope with was all the publicity afterwards. I would have been much happier for it all to have gone away.

Lisa: How did it affect your family?

Graham: Oh, they loved it! I've got to be honest, the girls loved it. They laugh about it now. My family in Australia all thought it was great. It's like everything, if you're not there, and you don't know the ins and outs. It does look quite fun on the video. I've got to be honest, it does look good and they did a good job and I had a really good time with the BBC and the crew.

They say that everybody has fifteen minutes of fame – I'd have settled for fifteen minutes, certainly, but I wasn't pleased that it was a lot longer. I still cringe. I was standing in the middle of the road the other day and somebody shouted out, 'Ah! It's the hero!' I hate it.

Lisa: You helped to save three lives, that's the important thing to remember. 'And he who saves one life, saves the world entire.'

Lisa's Reflections

I think Graham really was a hero, and deserved his award. It *is* funny that it all happened on 1 April, April Fools' Day, and that he fell in the water, but I still think he was seriously brave. He may not have meant to dive into the freezing cold water, but he could easily have decided to get himself straight out again. He didn't even think of doing that. He went on thinking about the danger the boys were in, and trying to help them. He swam to join them between the submarines, which he knew could have swung together at any moment and crushed him or drowned him along with the boys in their boat. He knew the danger they were in much better than they did, and he didn't hesitate to go and be with them to help keep their boat steady, and to keep them calm until they could be pulled to safety.

He told me that he was thinking of his daughters – he dearly loves his daughters and he has sent me pictures of them since I went down to interview him. He had a natural father's instincts, wanting to protect the young, and also he did think the boys were much younger than they actually were.

But the reason the press called him a hero was because they thought he'd dived in to save the three boys. And nothing he could do or say would stop them from believing that. As he said, if he'd not fallen in by mistake, the rescue would have happened and nobody would have thought anything more about it. Perhaps there would just have been two or three lines at the bottom of page five in the local paper.

I thought it was funny when I asked him if his wife and daughters were proud of him and he said, 'Well they are. And that's the other thing that's annoying, because I've said to them, "Well! Here you are, you're proud – and I just feel a fool." ' That did make me laugh. He was quite indignant with them.

I know Graham finds the whole thing dreadfully embarrassing. Even at Christmas, after I'd done the interview, he put on his card, 'You aren't really going to put my interview in your book, are you, Lisa?'

I think he's funny, I think he's lovely, I think his story is funny, and I also think he's every inch a true hero.

9

Mary Blake
– Dunblane Primary School

13 March 1996

Mary Blake wrote to me in September 1998. I was just
going back to the hospital for another operation, and I
can remember opening the letter and crying because all
of a sudden there was somebody out there who I felt
could understand me. I could talk to the people at my
school, but nobody had been so directly involved. Mary's
letter gave me a wonderful feeling of support – I felt a bit
better. I had someone I could talk to who would understand. Not so alone.

What happened at Dunblane Primary School in March
1996 and what happened at St Luke's three months later
affected not just us. Nearly everyone in the country –
every little child, every mother and father, every grand-
parent – has been terrified and suffered with us in their
mind over what happened. What did happen was worse
than anybody's worst nightmare. I can vividly remember
watching Dunblane on the news; I couldn't stop watching

and crying. I thought it was a tragedy, but I thought that it was a complete aberration that could never ever happen again. Three months later my own little nursery school was under attack from another madman. The world feels a less safe place since 1996.

Mary's Story

We've lived in Dunblane for twenty-three years. We've got three children. One son has left home, but he comes back home for his washing. My other son and daughter are still living at home.

I was in Dunblane Primary for nine years. I wasn't a teacher. I was involved with helping children with special needs. I worked full time, from nine until three thirty. For a long time I was involved with one particular child who had visual impairment. I was responsible for her books, enlarging the print for her books – and making sure she could see what was on the blackboard – anything to do with her sight.

By the beginning of 1996 she was in Primary 7, and we thought that it was better for her to have a wee bit of independence. Primary 7 means she was eleven or twelve years old and I'd been with her since she was six or seven. So at the beginning of the new term in August1995 we decided we would give her a bit more space and give her time, to see how she coped on her own. So then I was just helping out generally in various classrooms.

From January 1996 I was in Mrs Mayor's class for three days a week. They were Primary 1/13, so they were mainly five-year-olds, and a few six-year-olds. The school is for children right up to the time they go to high school. It's a big school, one of the biggest primary schools in Scotland, although now it's been made into two schools. When I was there, there were over six hundred pupils.

It was about a five-minute walk along to the school

from my home. And that particular morning it was cold and frosty, but quite bright. I remember I had a new blouse on that I'd bought at the weekend and my family had said, 'Oh, you look very smart today!'

My daughter was at the high school, and one of my boys had gone off to work, and Alan, my oldest, was at home because he had taken the day off. And my husband Frank was at home because he hadn't been well.

I left the house at about ten to nine, went off to school, got to the cloakroom and hung up my coat, and went along to Gwen Mayor's classroom. The children were all lined up in the classroom, with their gym kit on. And I couldn't for the life of me think why, because the gym lesson wasn't until half past nine. I spoke to Gwen, and she said that we'd all forgotten that it was assembly that morning, at nine o'clock, and she'd got them into their gym kit 'so that we don't waste time'.

Assembly was at nine o'clock in the main hall. I wasn't needed for assembly, so I went through to the staff room where I was enlarging some more books for the other child that I looked after. I kept a stock of stuff for her. I got to the staff room and then I suddenly remembered that I'd left my handbag up in Mrs Mayor's classroom. So I went back and collected my handbag and I spoke to the teacher from the next-door classroom, because she had also forgotten that it was assembly. Because it was such a big school, the assembly hall was not large enough for all the school at one time, so the assemblies were done in rotation. On this day it was for all Primary 1, 2 and 3 classes. I just said to her, 'Och well!' because we did all sometimes forget.

Then I just went back to the staff room and sat there working for the next twenty-five minutes. I kept looking up, because from where I was sitting I could see when they came out of assembly. And when I saw the minister coming out, I went across to the gym, which was behind the main hall. I arrived there before the class did, so I spoke to Eileen Harrild, the PE teacher, and we chatted for a couple of minutes until the children came along from assembly.

Mrs Mayor came along with them, and the three of us spoke together for a couple of minutes and then Eileen was busy with the children, and Gwen and I sat down on a bench just inside the door.

Eileen was telling the children not to touch the apparatus that was out in the gym that day at the far end, because they were too young to use it on their own. They had to have supervision. While Eileen was talking to the class in the middle of the gym, Gwen and I sat and talked about the morning's work. Gwen was about to go off to a meeting, and another teacher was coming to take the class after gym. And with the rush in the morning, forgetting about assembly and getting ready for the meeting and so on, I don't think she'd had time to leave things out on her desk for the rest of the morning. So she was telling me what was going to happen.

I just happened to glance up and one of the children was slightly misbehaving. I got up to keep the peace, and to check what was happening. I said to Gwen, 'I'll just be a minute.'

So I got up to go over, and even before I had reached the child I heard a loud noise, and then the door opened . . . And the next thing was, I was on the floor. It just happened so quickly. It was unbelievable how quickly it happened. I thought it was somebody having a joke. I couldn't believe what was happening.

I was shot in the leg, and I fell just where I was, in front of the benches. Gwen was shot.

I think the first sound I'd heard must have been when he'd been in the main hall, which was just behind the gym, and had fired shots into the stage. I don't know why. Perhaps it was just frustration, knowing that he had missed the assembly, because there would have been two or three hundred children there and I think he was perhaps hoping to get them all.

I was on the floor and I honestly don't know how I got up, but I managed to get up, and I think it was then that I was shot in the head, because suddenly there was just a – I don't know . . . I imagine it was something like being in an explosion. I heard the children crying, and it was really as though the sound of their crying was inside my head. However, I stood up again – how, I'll never know, but I did. There was some equipment kept in a store cupboard at the back of the gym, a sort of recess, where they kept the balls and the bats and a lot of outdoor equipment, and I was aware of Eileen crawling past me and going in there. To be honest I was really disorientated and I couldn't focus properly. I couldn't think – I just couldn't think what was happening.

By this time some of the children who weren't badly injured had rushed over to me, because I was the only adult standing. How I managed to push them in front of me I'll never know, but we all got into this recess behind Eileen. I didn't work any of this out. I didn't go away out and gather them all up. The children were just there in front of me and I said, 'Come on, come on, quickly – follow Eileen,' and pushed them into the recess.

So I did that, and I can remember just slumping down on top of some goalposts. I didn't realise until I was in hospital later that I was literally just black and blue, from the way I'd fallen on top of these goalposts. I think there were four children in the recess with us. Two were lying on top of Eileen and myself. Eileen had been shot – we didn't know how badly. Blood was coming from her chest and arms and I could feel blood trickling down the back of my neck.

So we were all just lying there. Some of the children were quite badly injured, I could see the bullet holes in their arms, their legs, and I remember putting my finger up to my lips to shush them. We all had to keep so quiet, because he could have seen us. We had no protection, because there was no door to this recess.

The kids were great. They seemed to realise the danger we were in. It only lasted three or four minutes, but it seemed like a lifetime. The noise, and the smell of blood and fear, were dreadful. Then there was a lull, when he went outside and shot up the library and the Primary 7 hut, but luckily Catherine Gordon, the Primary 7 teacher, saw and heard him and told the class to get down on the floor – just in time. And then he came back in the gym again. He was firing shots all round the gym while we crouched in the recess.

I thought that was it – we weren't going to survive. My thoughts were with my family. Frank hadn't been well and I kept worrying about what this would do to him. And how the children would cope without me.

There was just this terrible noise of gunfire. Then there was silence. I don't know for how long. A couple of minutes perhaps. Maybe a bit longer. I can't remember. By this time I was really drifting in and out of conscious-ness. But I do remember that some of the children stood up, and I wanted to but couldn't find the strength to say, 'Get back.' But I thought, 'If he's still hanging about and he sees these children, he'll kill them.'

Then one of the children said, 'He's gone.' And one of the wee ones lying on top of us kept saying, 'What a bad man. What a bad man.' He was very badly injured.

I didn't know that the man had shot himself. I didn't know fifteen of the children in the gym were already dead. And although I'd seen Gwen lying slumped on the bench, I didn't know that she was dead. I just didn't think that could have happened. It was like a dream. But I also didn't think for one minute that we were going to get out of there alive.

Anyway, the children got up and were milling round, and I didn't have the strength to tell them to lie down, keep quiet and stay hidden. Some of them went off to investigate. They were found by the janitor, who had heard the shots. I don't know where they were taken after that. Quite a few of them who hadn't been badly injured had actually got up and gone out of the school. I was still waiting for the man to come round that corner and shoot at us again. There were bullet holes just near where we were, so he must have been shooting right at our recess.

I don't know if I felt fear exactly. I think it was just like a dream. It was all in slow motion. It was incredible. It seemed an age before anybody came. It was the nursery teacher who I remember seeing first, and my first thought was, 'Oh, thank God! Somebody's found us. And whatever it was – it must be over.'

I don't really remember what happened then. A great number of people were coming backwards and forwards. I was beginning to slip in and out of consciousness again. I can't remember what I felt. I couldn't feel my legs, they were absolutely numb, and I could feel there were bullets in both sides. I could feel the blood running down my neck. I was scared to put my hand up to my head, because I honestly thought that the back of my head was away. It felt so sore and it was as if there was an awful noise inside my head.

The doctors arrived from the local health centre and attended to us. I remember I had got hold of some kitchen paper and put it onto my head. I was quite exhausted and couldn't think what to do. I knew I really should be holding my head, but I just couldn't bear to . . . anyway, the doctors came, two of them, and it was just great to see them. One of the lady doctors was really shocked. They all were. It was so terrible. But by then we had begun to have a wee bit of hope that the worst was over.

Then the emergency services arrived. I can hardly believe it, but the whole thing must have taken place between twenty-five to ten and twenty to ten. By quarter past ten we were all in ambulances being taken to hospital. I do remember when I was being taken out to the ambulance wondering what had happened to the gunman, and I kept thinking, 'What if he goes to the high school? My daughter's in the high school.' These things flash into your mind, and of course, I didn't know he was dead by this time. I wish I had known. I always dread the sound of the sirens – I absolutely hate it. There was just Eileen and myself in one ambulance. We didn't talk. I don't think I was even conscious most of the time. It's only six miles from the school, but it seemed to take forever. I remember the ambulance stopping at the hospital when we arrived, but very little after that.

You can't think it's happening. It's like a nightmare. I kept thinking it was some kind of joke. I was taken along to surgery. The nurses at the hospital were asking me questions, and I remember one of the nurses taking the scissors to my new skirt and blouse. While I was still at the school I could see that where the bullets had gone into my leg, my tights were all torn, and I kept thinking, 'My tights are in a terrible mess.' You can't take in the enormous things. Your mind shuts down. It's as though you can only think of these stupid things.

They cleaned out all my wounds, and removed the bullets. I had a bullet in the side of my head. It missed my brain. And I had one in one thigh and two in the other one. Four bullet wounds. When I was lying in the recess in the gym, seeing these bullet holes, I couldn't believe I was looking at my own leg.

It was sore and very painful, and my head still feels quite weird to the touch. My leg from the knee to the scar still feels numb. At the beginning I couldn't even feel pins and needles. But gradually I felt a bit of sensation, although even now I can't tell if I'm touching my leg. But really my head has given me the most trouble, because it is constantly sore.

I was taken out of theatre and into intensive care for a wee while, and then into a recovery ward. Frank was there when I came out of theatre, and I don't remember, but I think I was asking where he was, the gunman, and who he was. And then I don't remember anything else until I was back up in a ward. Frank and the kids were there, and they were all really shocked when they saw me – especially my daughter, Alison, because I was covered in foil, to keep the heat in, and of course I had an oxygen mask and I had a couple of drips. My whole face was swollen. It's not nice seeing anybody like that, but when it's your own mother, it must be quite frightening.

I was kept that night in the High Dependency Unit. I don't remember an awful lot about that night, except I was really, really sick. I think it was the effect of the anaesthetic. A friend who works in the hospital came in to see me, and she had to keep giving me bowls to be sick in! It's very hazy, all that first night.

The day after that I was speaking to one of the surgeons – they were wonderful, absolutely wonderful, they couldn't do enough. They both kept coming in and talking to me. I felt so terribly guilty, when I knew that the children had lost their lives and I was still alive. I didn't know at first that there were so many.

When I was able to talk with one of the surgeons again on the Friday, I had this dreadful feeling of guilt.

He kept telling me, 'You've lost four pints of blood. If you'd lost any more you wouldn't have been here. You'd have been a fatality as well. What else could you have done? With a madman with a gun? There's nothing you could have done.' It was good to talk to him and just be reassured I suppose. I just couldn't come to terms with the whole thing.

I find it all so difficult. I shall always find Mother's Day difficult, and any day if it's a Wednesday the thirteenth, it doesn't matter which month it is, I find that so hard. I think in time it will probably wear off, but you feel so many different emotions. Probably over the weekend, you know, gradually I was told how many of the children had died. I don't know if I wanted to know. I don't remember asking – I was trying to blot it out.

And although I suppose I knew deep down that Gwen was dead, I couldn't accept it. On the Friday I was wheeled into Eileen's room, because our wards were back to back. It was the first time I'd seen her since the incident, and she confirmed that Gwen had died.

There were twenty-eight children in the class. Two were absent that day. Sixteen were killed. All the rest except for two had injuries. But then, even the ones that weren't injured, they were there, and saw what happened. They were all injured in that way.

There was a policeman on guard on the ward, between Eileen's room and my own room, which was reassuring. I felt so frightened. I was scared out of my life. I obviously knew by that time that Thomas Hamilton was dead, but I was still so frightened. I don't know why really.

The nurse came in with a basket of flowers and when I looked at the note, I remember saying, 'These aren't for me. I don't know anyone of that name.'

'No, they are for you,' she said. 'There's one for Eileen as well.' Then it suddenly clicked they were from a well-wisher. And then gradually the room was absolutely filled out with flowers. The nurse was saying, 'There are no vases for them all.'

And I had cards and letters. In fact there was one from two young men who flew down from Aberdeen on the Saturday just to deliver flowers to us. I didn't see them because I was in theatre that morning. Oh, it was incredible. It helped to know that so many people were thinking about us. There was so much feeling. And Frank kept dropping in and bringing more and more presents.

Lisa: I can remember watching it all on the news and we put a candle in our church. A little white candle, for the teacher and for all the children that had been injured. I remember watching it over and over again on the news.

Mary: Yes, I remember somebody else saying that to me, somebody who didn't have children at the school, but she said how she couldn't stop watching, trying to realise that it had actually happened. We were in hospital, and we were really detached from that part of it. We didn't see any television or newspapers or anything. People kept telling us about all the flowers that were lined along the road, from the school entrance, right the way down the road, absolutely covered, blanketed, you couldn't walk on the pavement, it was all so covered in flowers. Eight days later they were being taken away on the Thursday night. I was being discharged from the hospital on that Thursday, and there are two ways we can come. I decided we would come the way that we would see all the flowers. The kids said, 'Oh, I don't think you should, Mum, it will upset you.' But I said, 'No, I feel I should see them.' It was upsetting but it was also incredible.

Lisa: Does the press attention still come back to Dunblane now, four years on?

Mary: Yes. Every time another incident — if anything happens. Another shooting or anything — they always phone us to get our comments about it. When the Columbine High School shooting happened in America, they were on the phone here. People from there are coming to Scotland in March of this year to meet up with some of the families affected in the Dunblane shooting.

Lisa: When you came out of hospital — could you walk?

Mary: I could walk, yes, so-so. I couldn't manage the stairs all that well. Once the stitches were taken out after another week, that helped a bit. The family were all at home with me. Both the boys had time off work, and Alison was at school, but she took time off school. They were all very good. They wanted to be with me and I couldn't face going out — I didn't leave the house for a fortnight.

The press were at the door for the first two or three days. In fact there was a camera out there focussing right down onto the house. We had a wee bit of knocking on the door, but I don't think it was too bad. Loads of phone calls and so on. I spoke to a reporter once in the hospital, but I didn't realise that it was going to be for television. I thought it was for the local paper, and then the camera came into the room.

That was for the television news on Friday night. They came again on the Sunday, which was actually Mothering Sunday, and the Queen was coming. She was in Dunblane that day, and she came to visit us in the hospital in Stirling as well. My hair was in such a mess — because obviously I had been shot in the head so nobody had touched it —

and my hair was all matted and horrible. I asked my son to ask my friend to bring in a hot brush or something to try to do something with it. Alan phoned my friend and said, 'Can you try and do something for my mum's hair because the Queen is coming?' So her husband arranged for a hairdresser to come into the hospital on the Sunday morning. She washed my hair and dried it, and oh it felt so much better.

We were wheeled downstairs near the children's ward, and she came in and Princess Anne was there as well. They spoke to us all, and to the kids. So that was quite nice.

And John Major and his wife Norma came, and Tony Blair and his wife as well. They came on the Friday. Some of the kids from school came to the hospital to visit us. John Major was really nice. So concerned and he knew all about my injuries and where they were and everything. He was really genned up. Tony Blair was just in total shock. And Cherie. Of course they have young children.

Lisa: It affected people all over the world. When did you find out that you'd got the Queen's Commendation for Bravery?

Mary: Oh, it was quite strange. Eileen phoned one morning and said, 'Did you get your letter?'

I said, 'No, our post hasn't arrived yet. What letter?'

'Oh,' she said, 'I wish I hadn't said anything.'

'But what is it?'

'It's a letter from St James's Palace, to say that we have been awarded the Queen's Commendation for Bravery.' And I just started to cry, standing in the hall, and just then the post came, and I said, 'Hold on, here's the post.' And the letter was there. I was crying and I didn't know what to think, so I think I said, 'I'll phone you back later and I'll just try and compose myself.'

We were told not to say anything. Then we were told when it was, 9 July 1997. The Queen was up in Edinburgh. It was a beautiful day, absolutely gorgeous and we were invited to Holyrood Palace, and Frank and my three children went as well. We were sent a stretch limousine, and it was a beautiful day.

Again, there were a lot of mixed emotions. Mrs Mayor got a posthumous commendation. Honestly, I didn't know how the families who had lost their children and the families with injured children – I wasn't sure how they would react. Then, the night before we went, one of the families who had lost their child came to the door with a beautiful bouquet of flowers. You've no idea how that made me feel. That was really one of the nicest things. It was as good as getting the award, it was so . . . This particular family had lost their child, but they were big enough and thoughtful enough not to forget about us.

We had such mixed feelings – it was a difficult day. It was a nice day but also very difficult and the children were very much in our thoughts. You just couldn't get away from it, knowing why we were getting it – we would so much rather not have been there in the first place.

There was no great big celebration or anything. Our two families, my family and Eileen's family, just went and had a quiet meal. The press were at Holyrood Palace, then they left us and that was it, we weren't bothered by them again.

I don't feel that I did anything. We tried to keep the children quiet as best we could. That was all. What can you do against a madman with a gun? I don't think I did anything brave. My great regret is that we had to lose so many children. But there's nothing more we could have done. We did our best, and got our group of children to keep quiet, and hopefully it meant he didn't come and find them. But nothing can make up for what happened that day. It was just appalling. My heart bleeds for the parents who lost their children. Nobody can know how they feel, however hard they try.

Lisa: When did you actually return to the school?

Mary: The school reopened probably about a fortnight later. Just under a fortnight. It was coming up to the Easter holidays. The staff went back – although they weren't teaching they were in the school, just having meetings and discussions. It couldn't have been easy for them going back.

It was quite a wee while – it would be a few months before I eventually plucked up the courage to go back. There was a couple of times I thought, 'Right, I'll go.' I wasn't going on my own, there was somebody to take me. And at the last minute I reneged, I just couldn't face it. Eventually I went one night when the school was closed, just to have a look at where the gym had been. The gym had been taken down by then. It was taken down practically straight away.

It's lovely now, it really is. There's a little flower garden. The school's been refurbished, and it all looks totally different. I can still see the gym in my mind . . . but it's not as it was.

I didn't ever go back to work there. I always felt apprehensive about it. It wasn't a nice feeling. And even yet, if I do visit the school, I don't enjoy it.

Lisa: I had six months off for my injuries, and then I went through the court case, and then returned to the school in January 1997, and I remember going back into the nursery and seeing a tiny bloodstain on the side of the mirror and just thinking, 'I want to be out of here.'

And every day when I went to the school, I didn't want to be there. I literally had to drag myself out of bed. My mum used to say, 'Don't go.'

But I used to think, 'I'm going to beat this.' But it got to the point where I couldn't eat properly. I was in such a state, and it was then that I started to have a lot of flashbacks. The first time it struck me was when I was in the playground – you know how children scream when they are playing? – I thought, I can see it all happening again. It was so vivid in my head it was like it was actually happening again. I just said, 'Can I go home?'

Mary: I really did think I would go back at the time, but eventually decided I couldn't cope. A couple of years later I got a transfer to the new school, but I only worked there for about six weeks. I just didn't feel comfortable.

Although the new school is completely different from Dunblane Primary – perhaps it was just the school environment. I felt apprehensive all the time. I didn't like going into the hall, even though their gym hall was completely different from Dunblane, but I still couldn't feel comfortable.

Lisa: *Was the first anniversary very hard? I remember hating that day. At half past three I wanted to be miles away.*

Mary: That was very difficult, yes. We were dreading it. The first year was traumatic. But in fact I think the second anniversary was even worse. The first year I think we were all so busy with the snowdrop petition, banning the guns, and generally being busy. Although it was still awful, by the second year things had quietened down and I had more time to reflect. And that was worse. On the first year, every family lit a candle in the evening at seven o'clock and put it in the window, and I think perhaps the whole of the community did the same, just to remember.

There had been a remembrance service, but that was in the October of 1996, before the anniversary. Prince Charles came to that. That was a difficult day as well.

We've had a lot of difficult times, and of course the first Christmas, that passed in a blur. Everyone just tried not to think about it. The magic had gone out of Christmas. I had always loved Christmas before.

Lisa: Do you feel like a different person?

Mary: I think it's changed me a little. There isn't anything specific. I think you get things into perspective. You feel like you've been robbed of something.

Lisa: I feel I've lost being young. Did you have counselling or anything to help you?

Mary: I saw a psychologist, but this was much later, after a year. At the beginning we were each assigned a social worker. But I had said from the first that I didn't want a social worker. I wasn't ready to start talking to a strange person. I had enough people, my local doctor was a friend as well as my doctor, and I knew I could talk to him if ever I felt I wanted to talk to anybody. I wanted to be left alone with my family, my friends and the people who were involved in the tragedy. I didn't want to talk to anybody else, and so I had said that I didn't want a social worker. But this lady was thrust upon us really, which I found quite distressing at times.

At the beginning of 1997, I did see a psychologist. My doctor recommended that I perhaps should see somebody. At that stage I probably was thinking myself that I should talk to somebody, but when it was coming close to the time of my appointment I really wasn't looking forward to it.

The first two or three times I found it so hard to talk.

I'm not all that good at expressing my feelings. But gradually, as I got to know him, it was fine. And it was good to know I wasn't going off my head or anything. I used to have a nice chat with him, and he was very supportive as well. I've now stopped seeing him, but I felt it helped a lot.

I'm beginning to sleep better now, I think. But for the first few years, I always woke up during the night. I still get flashbacks. Certain things will bring it on. Even a smell, or just different noises. A year, a year and a half ago, I was driving down past the school, and it was nearly starting time, and there were quite a few children with their red sweatshirts on, and that really upset me. I could visualise the classroom the way we'd left it that morning, with all the wee red sweatshirts on the desks. It's just silly things that bring it back.

Sudden noises I hate. Even the sound of children screeching still unnerves me a bit. Nobody knows. The first time I went shopping on my own, I just couldn't concentrate on what I was doing. I bought all sorts of rubbish. I felt I had to begin to do something for myself. I'd always had somebody with me. But I felt so apprehensive and weird, I just wandered round like a zombie with my head down.

Anyway, after I had done it, I felt a bit better. And the next time wasn't quite so difficult.

Lisa: *It's amazing, really, the amount of courage and strength it takes to get back to doing normal things like that.*

Mary: I know. It's everyday things. I used to get frustrated and angry about it. How dare somebody come and disrupt my life. Not to be able to go shopping without worrying about it. I still can't sit in a cafeteria with my back to the door. I've got to see the door.

Lisa: *I remember the first time we met in Edinburgh after you wrote to me, it was the way we both sat at the table, I sat here, you sat there, so we could both see the door and have our backs to the wall. Then some woman dropped her tray and we both jumped. But it was so good to meet someone who felt just like I did.*

Mary: I think everybody needs a bit of support. I knew that if I had been the only person involved in the gym that day, I really would feel quite isolated.

As it was, there were two of us, and Eileen and I could talk to each other about things that other people couldn't understand. How could they? They weren't there. We could discuss things that we couldn't even discuss with our own families.

And meeting the bereaved families did help a lot as well. They had meetings once a week and we were invited. So we got to know the parents. We didn't know them before – I didn't know them before. We know them very well now. And I do the same with the injured families. They had a focus meeting, and we got to know them. We still see some of the children – really growing up now. They were five and six, so they are quite big now. Nine- and ten-year-olds. It's sad, because you think of the children who aren't here, and wonder what they would be like now.

Lisa: *People quite often say, 'Are you over it now?' I think I will probably come to terms with it, and I have come to terms with it quite a lot, but it will always be there. You don't ever get completely over it.*

Mary: That's right. It's still very raw after nearly four years. The time has flown so quickly. It just seems like the other day. It will get better. But I don't think I've really come to terms with it yet. Not fully. And – I'm talking about it just now – but I feel quite detached from the whole thing. It's as though I'm talking about somebody else. I can't believe that it actually happened. I go to the cemetery from time to time and standing there you just can't believe that these children are there, and you'll never see them again.

Lisa's Reflections

Talking to all the people in this book has helped me, above all talking to Mary, because her experience was so close to my own. My little Francesca still talks to me about the man at our school – why did he do it? But I haven't got an adult to talk to about it, who was actually there. But talking to Mary over the past year has been nearly as good.

She talked about being so frightened all the time she was in hospital, even though she knew Thomas Hamilton was dead. I was frightened for weeks. I was frightened first of all because he was on the run for a time and I thought he would come and get me. I knew he wouldn't but I was still afraid. My mum and dad were there and there were flowers and cards and everybody around me and I thought, 'I'm not going to tell anybody that I'm scared he might come.'

I think everyone remembers the pictures of the mountains of flowers and teddy bears at Dunblane. It was like when Princess Diana died. People all over the world felt they had lost a beautiful friend, and at Dunblane, people from the other side of the world felt they had lost those children. I remember watching the pictures of Dunblane on the news, and thinking, 'This is not the world I live in.'

People have said to me, about what happened to me, 'Are you over it now? Is it all done?' I wish it were. Like

Mary, I have still got a long way to go. All the people in the book who have told you their story, including me, have to heal and go through many different stages before we will become completely whole people again. Some people may do it over a year – for people like Mary it may take a lifetime.

10

Euan Duncan
– Unsung Hero of Everest

Everest Expedition

April – June 1996

I first met Euan Duncan at the RADAR People of the
Year awards of 1997, the year after I got mine. I didn't
have the chance to talk to him much that evening, but I
heard his story, and when I was thinking about this book
he was one of the people whose addresses I asked Bert
Massie, the Managing Director of RADAR, to send me,
which he kindly did. By then Euan was travelling all over
the world, and it took some time to track him down.

When I finally got hold of Euan, back from his travels,
he invited me to go as his partner to the May ball at his
RAF station in Lincolnshire. It was a good three-hour
drive from my home, on a beautifully sunny day. Everything there was organised on military lines, everything
done perfectly to time, and the tables all laid out with
white tablecloths and flowers.

We went to the ball, and late that night we found a quiet room and did the interview while the music played on and the dancing continued outside. We must have talked until nearly two o'clock in the morning, me in my ball-gown, and Euan in his mess dress. Then I went off to bed in the guest quarters, and Euan carried on partying. When I played back the tape later I found that over some of the more dramatic bits of his story, I could hear background sounds of laughter and clinking glasses.

His story is rather different from all the rest in this book, because whereas the others were each faced with a totally unexpected situation, Euan was actively looking for a challenge, to test himself against the elements. To be honest, when we first started talking, I thought he was rather a hard man and a bit of a male chauvinist. I didn't think I was going to be able to relate to him as well as I could with some of the others. I thought he seemed cut off from what had really happened inside him, and from his own feelings. Which only goes to show that you shouldn't ever prejudge people.

As we talked I gradually realised that his bravado *was* something I could understand. I probably sometimes come across as rather a laughing, giggly person, because laughing helps me to let go of a lot of tension. My laughing is a way I get relief from too much emotion. And I came to see that behind his macho façade, Euan is a person who had suffered much more than he likes to admit. He said afterwards that nobody before had ever asked him about his story in such depth as I did that night.

I knew a bit about what had happened from the award ceremony, but until the night of the ball I hadn't realised how deeply it had affected him. To begin with he seemed quite detached. He began by telling me the story almost as though it was an adventure story that had happened to somebody else.

Euan's Story

I'm Flight Lieutenant Euan Duncan, and I was born on 2 October 1962. Born in Edinburgh, brought up in Hong Kong, joined the airforce at eighteen. Began life as an airman, worked my way through the ranks, got a degree, have served on four tours as an engineering officer. Currently based at RAF Coningsby. I will leave the RAF next year.

Everest has always been a childhood dream. It's something I've always wanted to do, but didn't think I ever would. Originally I just had this vision of climbing Mount Kilimanjaro, one of those hills you see in all those pictures, with the elephants and this big snow-capped mountain in the background. I eventually climbed that when I was at university. It was just short of 20,000 feet, and I climbed it and thought, 'That was good!' And then for some reason I thought, 'I want to go above 20,000 feet.' So I started looking round for other mountains to climb. Then I got the Seven Summits bug, the desire to climb all the seven highest summits on each of the seven continents. But it was still only a dream.

Then in 1990 I got posted to RAF Kinloss where I became the officer in charge. I joined the mountain rescue team, and that is where my serious mountaineering skills were honed. I was always a competent scrambler mountaineer, but two years of really professional training up in the Highlands gave me the ability to climb serious peaks, and that's when I realised that I could do more than I had originally thought I was capable of.

I went to South America in 1993 and 1994, and climbed Mount Aconcagua, which at 24,000 feet is the highest mountain outside the Himalayas. In 1995 I went to Alaska, to Mount McKinley and climbed that. The possibility of climbing all the seven summits suddenly seemed obtainable. I thought, 'Yeah. This might actually work.'

Then more by luck and chance than anything else I bumped into a very experienced Scottish climber, Mal Duff, in a pub of all places. We started chatting away and he told me he was putting together an international expedition to climb Everest in 1996. We went climbing together that weekend, and at the end of it he invited me to join his team, to go and try to climb Everest – so that is pretty much how I smoothed my way onto his expedition in 1996.

More by accident than design – the chance arrived. I grabbed it. I told the airforce that I wanted to go and do it. It costs about £25,000 per person to climb Everest. I was supported hugely by the airforce. But about £10,000 of it came out of my own life savings. And I was told in no uncertain terms by the airforce that I had to choose between mountaineering and engineering. I decided I'd go climbing. I'd have a crack at it. If I made it, I'd bring honour to the RAF and be the first airforce man to reach the summit of Everest. If I failed . . . Which is pretty much why I'm leaving the airforce next year as a flight lieutenant and nothing more.

I arrived in Base Camp on 1 April 1996. At that time of year Base Camp on Everest is like a thriving town or city. There are always lots of expeditions gathering there, getting ready to start humping their gear up to the higher camps, and they all have to be housed and fed and sold souvenirs.

There's a very short weather window on Everest. It generally starts around about 10 May. It can last for up to two or three weeks. Sometimes it only lasts two or three days.

The problem with Everest is that it is constantly hit by the jet stream. All the classical pictures you see of this plume coming off Everest, that's basically the upper level winds, called the jet stream, hitting the mountain. Then the jet stream drops to 29,000 feet – and you're talking 200-mile-an-hour winds and more hitting the side of the mountain. You just can't climb. You can't even stand or walk in it. But in the spring, as the monsoons move backwards and forwards and the weather changes, a ridge of high pressure moves in and pushes the jet stream upwards, so it clears Everest, and you don't have these ferocious winds going across the top. And that's your chance. You get in there, you climb, and you get out. In a good year there can be a two-week window when the jet stream is above the top of the mountain. But in 1996 it didn't happen. It was just one of those freak years. The jet stream never lifted off Everest for any length of time. Maybe just for a day or so at a time it sort of popped up and then came down again, but we never got our clear weather window. And we knew that. We were getting our weather reports by radio from Bracknell, and we knew it wasn't happening. We were going to have to go for a one- or two-day window if it happened at all.

Mal Duff was our expedition leader. His plan was to make a basically classic assault. You carry your gear up from Base Camp, which is at 17,000 feet, up to Camp One, at 21,000 feet. Camp Two was at 23,000 feet, and then you gradually have to sort of leapfrog up the mountainside. You've got to carry part of your gear up to a certain height, then come down and rest. Carry more kit, rest at Camp One, then you push on to the next camp, carrying more gear. Then you start moving your high-altitude gear, the oxygen and stuff, on up to Camp Three, and Camp Four and so on. So you actually climb the mountain, the total height, many times, but all you are doing is climbing up and down a little bit at a time. You make your final summit attempt from just under the highest ridge.

Our summit attempt was going to be on maybe 10 or

11 May, so we'd been there for six weeks before we would go for it. A lot of energy and strength had been expended already by then, humping our gear, getting up there. And it's mentally exhausting, just being at such a high altitude, seeing the summit you want to go to, but having to climb up so far with your gear, go back down, climb up again, go back. And much of this going backwards and forwards is across a massive icefall, a glacier flowing down the mountain, so it's really mentally draining. Everest's glacier is like a huge slide effect – the glacier slides downhill and then when it comes down to 20,000 feet it goes over a lip. You have to cross the Khumbu icefall, as big as a football pitch, always on the move, creaking and groaning and full of crevices and fissures, up and down three or four times before you've got all your gear up over it to the higher camps. But you can't even begin your summit attempt until that's done. It's potentially very dangerous and people have lost their lives there, before they have even begun the high-altitude climbing.

The day before our planned summit attempt, which was for 10 May, I was sitting with Mal at Camp Two, and we were formalising our plans to go. We had settled into teams. You work out who is climbing at the same pace as you, and try and put people together who work well together. I had ended up teamed with Mal Duff, the expedition leader, as climbing partner. That's the way it panned out.

Several other international expeditions, including ones led by Rob Hall and Scott Fischer were all pushing for the same sort of date to make their summit attempt. So we were all gathered at Camp Two, all our kit was in position, all the bases were prepared, all the oxygen and our high-altitude gear was already stashed at a high point at Camp Three, at about 25,000 feet. I'd already climbed it twice, left my gear, slept there, so everything was in place and we were ready to go.

Mal Duff's expedition was going a slightly different route from everybody else, but we would all have met up on the summit ridge around about the same day. Then Mal decided that perhaps that wasn't such a good idea because there would be too many people up there. He was a bit concerned, as was I, at the number of people who were going up there at the same time, and about the lack of experience of a number of people that were on the major expeditions. Rob Hall and Scott Fischer were taking a number of clients, many of whom were inexperienced climbers. These days, if you are rich enough, you can pay for Sherpas to practically carry you up Everest. Our own team was made up of all experienced climbers in our own right.

So we were a bit concerned about getting held up behind a big stream of inexperienced mountaineers, and we elected to haul off and wait for a day. But we decided to go out on a test run, see what conditions were like. It was 9 May.

We were wearing the sort of gear that you'd wear in the Scottish mountains, multiple layers of clothing. Underneath I was wearing silk thermal underwear – don't get excited now! Then I had three or four layers of clothing, then the old track suit, a fleece on top of that and then a windbreaker. My really expensive, heavy-duty gear – the big down jacket, down trousers and down gloves – was already stashed up with some oxygen at Camp Three, because I knew I wouldn't need it until then.

So what we had on was cold, but because we were moving relatively quickly we could survive in multiple layers. Once you got moving it wasn't too bad. First thing in the morning – we always had to get up at about two or three in the morning – the temperature was minus 50 degrees. But when the sun comes out it becomes fiercely hot. And that was the main problem. People think Everest is always cold, but it's not, it is actually boiling hot further down. On the Western Cwym, the glacier just short of Camp Two is like a huge bowl of ice, and when the sun comes out it just bakes. There's nowhere to go. The UV's horrendous. You can't hide in the tent because it's too hot. You can't lie outside because you burn. It's actually a thoroughly miserable place. It took me by surprise when I got there. I didn't realise it was going to be like that.

But anyway, you dress for the occasion, you've got multiple layers on and you can peel them off as the day goes on. But even though it is hot, it's freezing cold as well, and if you're not moving fast enough to keep warm, you've got to wear multiple layers all the time. But if you're an experienced mountaineer, you know what layers to wear, and it's not a problem.

That day Mal and I got to about halfway up what's called the Lhotse Face. We'd got there really quite early, maybe three or four o'clock in the morning, and we stopped about halfway up the face, and we looked at the weather and we looked at each other and said, 'This isn't really working. We don't want to be here. Maybe the weather is going to lift tomorrow.'

From where we were we could see the summit of Everest and that the jet stream hadn't really lifted. Where we were it was clear and fine. But what we could see above us, about seven or eight thousand feet above us, was the wind, and it was just whipping across the top of the hill.

We decided that for us it wasn't right. Mal wasn't comfortable, I wasn't comfortable and we said, 'Right, no. Today's not the day. No. We'll kiss it off. We'll go back to camp and wait.'

Rob Hall was a very, very experienced mountaineer. And there were a lot of people round about him, other expeditions, who all took a lead from Rob Hall. 'If Rob Hall's going, then we're going too.' He was the guru of Everest, quite frankly. Certainly the Taiwanese went on what he said, and the South Africans were basically waiting for what he did. Even Scott Fischer – although he was a very experienced Everest climber himself – to a degree he also wanted to see what Rob Hall did. Because Rob Hall was the main man.

We passed Rob Hall's and Scott Fischer's expeditions as we made our way back down, and they all went past us, going on up, and we said to them, 'We're going to call it a day. We're going back.'

And they said, 'We're going to press on.'

I'd talked to Rob Hall a couple of days earlier and he – it wouldn't be fair to call it a fixation – but he kept saying that 10 May was a lucky day for him. He'd gone to the summit with parties three or four times, and 10 May was his lucky talisman. Perhaps that clouded his judgment – well, I don't know. Who knows? At any rate, he pressed ahead. So they all pressed ahead. And on they went.

But we said, 'Nope. It's not for us. We're going back down because we're not happy.'

So we went back and sat down in Camp Two and just had a rest for the day.

And the next day, which was 10 May, the others all went for the summit. The weather was marginal, but they got there. But they were very slow getting there. There were a lot of problems on the route, getting the inexperienced climbers up there with the ropes. They had the problem that we had envisaged, of a lot of very slow climbers all trying to get up the same very narrow route.

Late that afternoon, nobody up there spotted it, but we could see it from where we were at Camp Two, a storm came rushing up the valley from behind them. We saw a lot of high winds whipping the snow up. And the cloud coming down – what would have normally been twenty-kilometre visibility came down to a few feet. When you are climbing up a mountainside, you tend not to look behind you. Especially when you are going for the summit – all you do is focus on the step ahead and the point you're going to get to. Nobody ever looks behind them. For the people who were climbing, they were looking in front, and ahead of them the skies were clear.

The first people must have reached the summit at about one o'clock. They reached the summit, turning round to look at the view, and as they turned round they could see in the distance this horrendous storm coming round the valley and up the hillside behind them. Uh-uh!

If you haven't reached the summit of Everest by very early afternoon, then you've got to go home, because you are not going to make it. It's going to get cold and dark and it's going to be difficult to find your tent back at your camp at night, especially when you're tired. So that is the experienced mountaineer's cut-off time, to be on the summit by two – maybe three o'clock in the afternoon at the very latest. If you are very quick and experienced, you can get on the summit by three and still get back down safely.

We saw the storm later that afternoon, and knew they were climbing, but we didn't think there was a major problem, because there were such experienced mountaineers leading them. By the time the storm would hit them, at five, six o'clockish, we thought they must all be down and inside their tents. There shouldn't be a problem.

We said to each other, 'Well that was a good decision. We'll go tomorrow.' We'd decided we were going to make our ascent the next day, on the chance that most people would be gone and out of the way by then. They would have broken the trail, and hopefully the weather would be right. So we just sat in the tent and waited for the next day.

But then we heard that they had all been reaching the summit very, very late. Rob Hall in particular didn't summit until very late, with his client, Doug Hanson. We knew this, because we'd heard it on the radio. One of the guys in our tent was a good friend of Rob Hall's, so he was listening in to their camp radio to see what was going on. And about ten o'clock at night he came across to the mess tent and said that Rob Hall had got a bit of a problem – he was very high up, with a client who was obviously ill, and obviously dying.

I thought, 'Well, that's not very clever. But OK, Rob Hall's experienced, he'll leave the guy, and he'll come off on his own.' Harsh reality – but if you can't look after yourself at that altitude, you are on your own. Rob Hall is sensible. He's been around a long time. So Mal and I went off to bed, concentrating on being ready to do our stuff the next morning.

We got up at about two the next morning to set off in good time, but we thought, 'Before we go, we'll just check in and see if Rob's all right, and if he needs anything taken up for him or whatever.' So we went in to Rob Hall's huge mess tent, which he had for all his clients at Camp Two, and there was just bedlam.

There were a number of people in there talking on their radio, and there were guys in tears. They said, 'Rob Hall's trapped.' He was below a place called the South Summit, which is very, very high up on Everest. It's probably round about 28,000 feet, I mean really high up. The climber he had taken up with him had died. People were on the radio to him, talking to him, just trying to get him to get up and move and walk away. But nothing was happening. I thought, 'OK, right. Somebody's got to go up and rescue him. Who knows what's going on?' Well, nobody did. He couldn't get up and walk apparently. He wouldn't leave his client. There were all sorts of problems.

Mal said, 'All right. We can wait another twenty-four hours to go for the summit. Let's make sure this guy gets off.' We tried to make radio contact with some people we knew were up there. But our radio didn't work. Everyone was using different signals and there was a sort of jam. At about daybreak I went to the South African tents to get their radios to try to get them to speak to somebody, but there was no information coming from anybody at the South Col, which was causing a bit of concern. Eventually we got some sort of radio contact with one of the tents and got a Sherpa, and one of our own Sherpas interpreted for him.

(Sherpas are like Sherpa Tensing, who climbed Everest with Sir Edmund Hilary. They are very low-paid, Nepalese high-altitude porters. They are very experienced local mountaineers and they are very, very good. Every expedition has to have Sherpas. They hump and dump all your large gear, otherwise us poor Brits would never get up there. We all have them. Our expedition had about twenty porters to get our gear to Base Camp and above that we had six or seven Sherpas to help us erect tents and carry our extra oxygen supply. But all our personal gear we had to carry ourselves. Which is why I went on Mal Duff's expedition because that's the way I wanted to climb the mountain. I wanted to carry my own personal gear. I wouldn't want some bloke carrying all my gear for me and just go up as a holiday maker. That's not mountaineering as far as I'm concerned.)

Anyway, we finally got hold of a Sherpa on the radio and asked him to find any European who was up there, and he said, 'There's nobody here.'

We said, 'What do you mean, there's nobody there? There are about forty people up there. What's going on?'

'No, this tent is empty. All the tents are empty.'

Eventually we got some European guy, whose name I can't remember. We got him on the radio and asked him what was going on. He said, 'There's nobody here. There are lots of people missing. There are bodies everywhere.'

We thought 'Shit!' Our radio kept giving out. The South Africans had a radio but they wouldn't give it to us, so we couldn't get a link down to anybody down below with a list of who was supposed to be up there. People in Base Camp were monitoring where everybody was, but up where we were at Camp Two we had no information.

We were trying to be a middle link to what was going on above us, but we couldn't get any sort of link system going. I was sitting with Mal Duff, with radios to Base Camp trying to get the names of people who they thought were up there. The guy in Base Camp had some kind of a radio link with some of the people on the South Col. We all tried to establish who *was* there, and who was actually missing, and eventually worked out that there was something like fourteen or fifteen people who were lost – nobody knew where the hell they were.

At that point we realised that we had a massive problem on our hands. We all knew the danger of being caught out at that sort of altitude and we realised straight away that people would have died. The guy on South Col had said, 'It's been blowing a gale out here all night.' And if you hadn't been in the shelter of your tent, then you would have been in serious, serious trouble. So we knew straight away that with that number of people scattered around, people were going to be dead or dying. We knew already that Doug Hanson, Rob Hall's client, had died because Rob had been on the radio. We spoke to Rob again at about five o'clock in the morning.

'Doug's gone' was basically what he said, and that's the last time he ever spoke about the bloke. So that was the

first casualty, and we knew there were going to be more
bodies. With that number of people lost on Everest at that
sort of height – you just knew.

There were six people in our tent at Camp Two. Two
Americans, the IMAX team, had been making a film that
year about climbing Everest. IMAX is a massive big screen.
I don't know if they've got them yet in the UK. They've
certainly got them in America and Australia. These guys
were experienced climbers anyway, and they were trying
to make a film that year on what it's like to try and climb
Everest. Henry Todd was another bloke who was there,
another British climber. So there was maybe half a dozen
of us in this tent at any one time.

So we thought, 'Right. We've got to organise something.
Let's sit down and try to organise our lives.' So we left
three or four of them on the radio talking to Rob, just
trying to keep him talking, cajoling him along, and Mal
and I went outside and thought, now what are we going
to do? We can get medical facilities up, get that sorted out.
Find out who is still up there, how many are still missing,
and try to get the guys down who can still walk down.

And we pretty much spent all day getting medical kit
brought up to Camp Two, where we were, from Base
Camp. A couple of guys came up with medical equipment.
We knew people would have come down with frostbite
and we would have to treat them where they were first,
before we could move them away. So we got a list of
people believed to be missing.

I don't think we ever panicked, because the situation
was already out of our control. I think you only panic if
you know you can do something about it quickly but
don't know what to do. We knew we couldn't do anything
about it quickly. All we could do was try for damage
limitation. We knew people had died, and that was going
to be a fact of life. We wanted to keep things moving, to

establish who was missing, where everybody was, and then help to bring off anybody who was still alive, and get them down.

High-altitude mountaineers tend to be rather phlegmatic in their attitude anyway. You panic more when it's life-threatening right in front of your face. But this wasn't threatening us.

We spent the whole of the next day getting organised. Then we began to bring people off. Quite a few had by now managed to struggle down under their own steam. Those that were still alive and capable of walking we got off, and got them to walk down that night. I think by the end of the first day there were still at least nine or ten people scattered around in various places, alive or dead. No trace of them whatsoever. Those that we got down we fed and looked after medically and tucked them away.

The first time contact was made with Rob there was a rescue package in hand. We had sent up food and oxygen from Camp Two. We knew where he was and two experienced Sherpas went to try and reach him to bring him down. It had to be somebody up at the South Col to go and get him.

At about two o'clock in the afternoon of 11 May, we got a radio call from the South Col and they said, 'The Sherpas are coming back now. We can see them coming down the hill.'

We said, 'How many?'

They said, 'Just two.'

'Where's Rob Hall?'

The jet stream had dropped down to below where he was, and you couldn't physically get up to him. The Sherpas had tried their hardest. And yes, they were paid to do it, but they respected him tremendously as a mountaineer. He was like a friend to them. He looked after them. He came back year after year with expeditions. So these

Sherpas would not have turned back from trying to get him if they had had any choice at all. They were on a mission to try and get him. But you can't fight a 250-miles-per-hour wind. It just couldn't be done.

When we got the news, we all just sat around in the mess tent. I could see them all, grown men, hard mountaineers, Mal Duff and Henry Todd and all these guys, just in tears because they knew then they couldn't get to one of their friends. He was talking to them on the radio, he was alive, and they couldn't get to him. That was heartbreaking. From where we were we could even see where he was – and we couldn't get to him.

And there was a fierce argument, I remember, in the mess tent, about what to tell him. The morality of the situation – right, what are we going to do now? Do we tell him the Sherpas are on the way, and just bullshit him until midnight, when he finally dies? Or do we tell him, 'You're on your own now. Get up and walk, or you're going to die.'

We never resolved it. It was going on and on – it got quite heated. Then thankfully, for everyone's sake, a close friend of his arrived from a nearby mountain. He'd heard about it over the radio the day before, he'd got wind that something serious was happening, and he had rocketed up to Base Camp, where he got on the radio to Rob Hall and basically told him, 'Sorry, mate. The rescue party couldn't get to you. You're on your own. If you're going to make it, get off your ass and walk.'

I remember that Rob's response was, 'If I could walk, I'd have walked out of here hours ago.' Different people kept on speaking to Rob Hall all day.

Then he said, 'I'm going off the air now for a while.' He just turned his radio off. And he did nothing for a few hours. Then he came back on the radio and said, 'This is Rob Hall here. Get my wife on the line.'

We patched a radio link to his wife in New Zealand. She knew what had happened by this time. They told her that the rescue party had failed, and while they were setting up the link to Rob, they started talking to him again, saying things like, 'How are you getting on?'

I don't want to hear this. The guy is dead. Effectively, he's a dead man now. We're not going to get to him. He's survived one night. He's frostbitten. He can't move. I couldn't listen. I just walked out of the mess tent and let them get on with it.

He talked to his wife about all sorts of things. His story has been told in various books. She was a climber too. They had met on a mountaineering expedition. I know one thing they talked about – she was pregnant with their unborn child and they named it. One or two of the guys stayed in the mess tent, but that wasn't the place for me. That was a dead guy talking to his wife. She knew it and he knew it. She'd been on Everest before. She was a doctor as well, so she knew exactly the situation he was in. They spoke for hours. It was phenomenal, the dignity of the man. Then we all spoke to him until about half past nine that night. Then he said, 'I'm going to sleep now.' He turned his radio off, and that was it. We never heard from him again. They found his body about two weeks later.

By that point it was desperately sad. There's no mandate to rescue people at that altitude. You are just relying on your friends to do what they can for you.

I don't know the exact numbers of people involved in the whole disaster. It was impossible to keep track of everybody. I started monitoring the numbers early on, but then it just got out of hand. And I got tied up with other things. One of the Sherpas took over and started logging people in and out, but it was almost impossible. Those who could walk came in by themselves, and then headed off and made their own way down to Base Camp. Some of them were exhausted, shocked and frostbitten, but they could walk, and they could survive, so they just got off the hill on their own. They'd had enough. They cleared off under their own steam.

The next day – it must have been 12 May by then – Mal and I went up from Camp Two to help the guides on South Col who were bringing down the ones who couldn't make it under their own steam. There were people up there who were completely exhausted and frostbitten, who had no energy to come down on their own.

We had gone to bed reasonably early the night before, because we were going out early. We started out at two in the morning, and climbed towards the summit, using the ropes they had left behind. We got the last survivor in at about eleven o'clock at night, and we were still on the go at one o'clock the next morning, so it was a twenty-three-hour day. It's amazing what adrenaline will do for you.

The Sherpas found Makalu Gau and hauled him off. That was a sad story in itself. They found Makalu Gau and Scott Fischer lying together in a snow grave. They gave oxygen to both of them. Makalu Gau revived enough to speak to them and showed signs that he could actually physically move. Scott Fischer was alive, no question about that, but he didn't recover enough to speak or move. So they took Makalu Gau, dragged him off the mountainside and left Scott there, and by the time they got back to him later he had died. But they could only rescue one person at a time with the facilities they had available to them.

Makalu Gau and Beck Weathers were both horrendously frostbitten and couldn't walk, so the Sherpas dragged them on sledges down to Camp One. The Nepalese pilot had stripped his Squirrel helicopter right down – it was working well beyond its limits, and I don't know how he ever got there – but he dropped in and managed to take Makalu and Beck one at a time down to Base Camp.

Thank God he did. There was no way they could have gone through the icefall on their own. The ice starts cracking and making fissures and crevasses as it flows down. These crevasses go down two or three or four hundred metres – just bottomless – and it's a natural flow like a river. It's a massive thing, with immense blocks of ice all over the place. And every night it moves, you can hear it cracking. So there was no way they could have got down there without being airlifted.

The problem with climbing Everest is you've only got one good crack at the summit. It's really debilitating living at that altitude, and as you expend energy keeping warm, your body virtually destroys itself. I lost three and a half stone during the time I was up there. And your body can only deal with that sort of abuse for so long. If on top of that you expend a lot of energy hauling people off from near the summit, then you've used up all your reserves. Mal and I both knew that if we went to haul people off, then we'd kissed off our chances of the summit.

So we realised that. At the time I didn't actually sit down and think, 'Gosh, that's me losing £10,000.' It was more like, 'All right, if we go and try and rescue some of these people, we're not going to reach the summit, are we? Nope.' We'd have a crack at it, but realistically we had pretty much had it. That was by the by. Main point is now, if we don't go up there and get them there's going to be another half a dozen bodies scattered about up there. The bottom line was there were people in trouble, people were dying, and if we didn't go and get them, they were stuffed.

Lisa: You say it exactly like I tell my story – I don't know if it's because I've told it over and over again. I find myself saying, 'This happened and then that happened' as if I wasn't talking about something quite horrendous, and you are doing the same thing.

Euan: I don't know if that – if this is our way of distancing ourselves from it? Perhaps that's our way of healing ourselves. Yes, it happened. Yes, we were involved in it. And yes, we were scarred by it to a greater or lesser degree, but if you are constantly agonising about it, you never heal yourself and never move on. But if you can somehow extract *yourself* from the fact that you were there – yes, we know you *were* there, but you have to try to remove the emotion from it.

Anyway, between us I think we got maybe a dozen guys down. One guy was Lou Kasischke. I remember clipping him into my harness, and his hands were so frostbitten he couldn't hold the rope or harness. He just hung there on my harness. I don't know if he'd lost any fingers, but you could tell they were frostbitten because they were solid. He certainly couldn't have come down the mountain on his own. To get down Everest you've got to clip yourself onto fixed ropes and haul yourself, and he couldn't. So I clipped him into my harness, and I did all the work for him.

There was Mal Duff ahead of me, and there were other climbers round about. I wasn't the only person there. Let's not get carried away and say '*I* saved fourteen people.' Because there were a lot of other people involved. There were guides who were still up there, from Scott Fischer's expedition. We were all bringing off people, anybody who was still alive. Anatoli Boukreev was a Russian guide up there, and he had already saved a couple of people before dawn on 10 May – Sandy Pittman and Charlotte Fox. He went out in the dark, in the blizzard, and hauled them back in to the camp. Anatoli was killed later, in December 1997, by an avalanche on Annapurna, another mountain in the Himalayas.

They had all managed somehow or other to get themselves back down to the South Col, which is somewhere about 26,000 feet, and there's a huge camp there, with tents and so on. It was from the South Col that they had gone up the West Ridge to the summit. Unfortunately half of them had still been on their way back down the same ridge when the storm came in, darkness hit, so they hadn't made it back to the tents. They had got caught out in various stages up and down the mountainside. But eventually, as dawn came in, most of them had stumbled in.

There were a lot of people there horribly frostbitten. Makalu Gau lost both his hands, both his feet, his nose, his ears, he was a mess when we got him back down. Lou Kashogi. Beck Weathers lost his hands – he lost one arm up to the elbow, the other up to the wrist. They looked like bits of charcoal, their noses. I've seen bitter frostbite, but never have I seen anything like that. It was just horrific. It was amazing they were still alive. But they were. Everybody who was alive, the morning we went up, came off alive. I think Beck Weathers was the last one we got back into Camp Two.

Lisa: *Did you ever think that your own life was at risk, helping these people?*

Euan: Your life is always at risk at that altitude. There but for the grace of God go I. If Mal and I hadn't turned round when we did, we would have been trying to get up to the summit at exactly the same time as they were. And we could have been in the same position, and I could be just another statistic today, one of the bodies scattered around the mountainside.

All right, I knew I was in danger, but I had been in danger before. I had resigned myself to the fact that this was a dangerous expedition – even before I left – you are going into a dangerous place. If things go wrong, you could die. That's a fact. If you don't want to take any risks, OK, don't go, stay at home and play tiddlywinks. But by making the decision to go and climb there, by definition you accept those risks. And you'll live with it.

The fact that we went up there to help the other people, OK, it was perhaps a little more dangerous, and we exposed ourselves to risk a little bit more. But you are too busy to think about that.

If the weather had been perfect, they'd have all summitted. We'd have summitted the next day, and gee, I'd have been the first person in the Royal Air Force to climb Mount Everest. I'd probably have been promoted. Well, things didn't pan out that way. It's no good thinking, 'What if?' You can't change it now. It's a waste of energy. I think about it a little bit, but I don't reminisce hugely. I don't feel . . . I may have been a bit depressed for a while. I don't know.

All I was really focussing on at the time was getting up there, and trying to get them down. You just climb, keep yourself as safe as possible, get up there. You are wondering what sort of state they will be in. Am I going to have to lower them in a plastic bag, tie them up? There was a huge vertical drop we had to lower them over. How am I going to get somebody over there? You are just trying to overcome all the practical problems in your mind, how you are going to deal with this or that problem. What happens if he slips here? It keeps your mind ticking over while you climb. How am I going to get over this? All the ropes are joined. There are little screw pickets in them. So every time you get to a certain point you've got to tie the rope off, go back down to him. Move the safety device.

Lower him down. Go back up. Get yours. So you are doing a lot of work for other people who can't grip for themselves. You have to just hope they can keep walking, one foot in front of the other. If they slip you hold them. They can't help themselves. Some of them were shellshocked.

Some were not so bad. They still had their oxygen masks. A couple of guys I spoke to said, 'This was supposed to be the adventure of a lifetime. It's been the worst nightmare of my life.' You could tell from their eyes that they had been through hell. Unless you've lived through it, you've no idea. Your tents are getting blown down. Once your tent has gone, you've no protection. You don't know if you will still be alive the next morning. It must have been a truly traumatic experience.

Once they realised there were people there to help them, you could see a great weight come off their shoulders. Somebody's going to help us. We're going to get home now. It's all over.

We took over all the worry for them. We had them safe. They just had to concentrate on walking. There were guys in tears. People in bits. They knew then that they'd finally get away. The weather was OK, but from where we picked them up it was still a long, long way to go, and if they had slipped and fallen on the way down on their own, they would have died. So they knew they were in trouble unless somebody came and got them.

They were walking off the mountain with what they stood up in. They had gone up with all sorts of gear. All the equipment, their rucksacks, sleeping bags, everything – they just left them. They didn't care. They just wanted to get off the hill, to get away.

Lisa: Were you frightened at all? Or is that a bit sissy to say?

Euan: I was concerned about the danger. There was always things coming down – rocks, ice – and we were aware that if you've got somebody heavy strapped to your harness, and they slipped, we could all get pulled off. But I think if you are frightened it means you've got too much time on your hands. We didn't have any time. All our time and energy was taken up and focussed on doing what we had to do to get them down. I didn't have any spare mental capacity to be frightened.

I wasn't doing anything that I didn't know how to do. I was professionally and skill-wise operating well within my training and ability. I knew what I was doing, I knew I was capable of doing what I had to do. It was high up and therefore dangerous, but the skills I was demonstrating were skills I had been trained in for several years, so it was second nature for me.

Once we had got them down to Camp Two we were up for most of the night. The worst thing was that some of them started to defrost. If you've got frostbite the best thing is to leave it frozen until you can get to a proper hospital. As your skin defrosts, all the cells are dead and so a lot of poison starts to seep back into your body, and then your liver and kidneys go into renal failure. Most people who die of frostbite die because of blood poisoning after defrosting. It's too much for the kidneys to cope with.

Unfortunately they had started to defrost on the way down, so we spent most of the night putting their hands in buckets, trying to warm them up gradually in lukewarm water, trying to thaw them out and at the same time to put lines of fluid into them intravenously.

Lisa: What about your dream of climbing to the summit?

Euan: Yes. Mal Duff and I discussed it afterwards. We had a good team, we were in a good position, everything was right, and we were climbing well together. Mal had been to Everest three or four times before but had never reached the summit. It was a dream of mine and a dream of his. Our dreams were there in the balance, and doing what we did, we had more or less put the skids under them. For me it was probably a chance in a lifetime. For Mal it was his life, his job, he was running a company doing that sort of thing. So he would get another chance, but he was still hugely disappointed, because this was probably the best opportunity he had had, because we made a good team.

Mal decided to take the whole team back to Base Camp to rest up for a week and then reassess the situation. I said, 'If I come back down to Base Camp, I don't think I'm mentally strong enough to come back up here again.'

Mal said, 'But you need to come back down for a rest.'

I said, 'No, well, I know the idea is get down low for a rest, build up stamina and climb high again, but if I go through the icefall again . . .'

I didn't think in my heart I'd be mentally strong enough to face going back down, and then coming back up. I thought, 'At the moment I'm up here. There's danger up here, and danger down there, but I'll just stay where I am'.

And that, in retrospect, was a very poor decision of mine. Based on inexperience, stupidity, whatever. I stayed up at 22,000 feet for almost three weeks, which is a horrendously long time. Your body cannot regenerate at above 20,000 or 21,000 feet. All your cells begin to die. If you cut your finger at that height, it won't heal up, your blood won't clot, you've got real problems. But I waited up there, more in hope than in anything else.

Unfortunately, your appetite just goes completely at high altitude, which is why you lose umpteen stone. We ate reasonably well down low at Base Camp, and the food was prepared for us and edible, but higher up you just weren't very interested, you didn't have the appetite or the heart for it. You have to physically force yourself to eat, because you know you need it for the energy. But you're not hungry. I usually live on choccy bars. Instant sugar is about the only thing you want to keep you going. So your energy comes from your body eating itself effectively, because if there's nothing in your stomach, the fastest source of energy for your body is muscle fibre. It can break that down into protein very quickly, and that will give you energy. At altitude you cannot physically take in enough calories to support the amount of energy you are burning up for the cold.

And the next stage is when your body starts to eat away all your muscle and fat, and you come back down like an Oxfam poster. And it's not pleasant, but that's where your energy comes from. That's why you have to be physically quite strong before you even go there. A lot of people are very fat before they go, because then they have some energy resources stashed away. They can live on their fat reserves.

But I still thought that if I went down low to rest and recover, the sadness and sense of apathy at base camp, with so many people having died, would affect me badly. And I was right. When we finally did come back down, two weeks later, the whole of Base Camp was deserted. After the disaster had happened, the heart had gone out of everybody. All the major expeditions had pulled out. That sort of accident will decimate a place. I knew that if I had gone down there I wouldn't have had the sort of determination, inner strength, inner will, to go back up and do it all again.

That's why I decided to stay where I was, quite high, and there were two or three of us did the same thing. I knew this was a dream. I knew my chances of making the summit were pretty remote now – but it was my only chance. I wouldn't ever come back.

So I made a conscious decision to stay and rest higher up. Mal and Henry Todd both tried to persuade me to come back down with them. I said, 'It's all very well for you saying that. You've been through the icefall several years on the trot. I don't think I've got the mental strength to do it.' Which is probably quite a weak thing to say, but I really don't think I did. I think I was pretty much pushed to the end of my tether by everything that had happened.

Unfortunately it wasn't a good decision, because I got more and more weak as the days went by. About a week later, on 18 May, Mal came back up with a couple of other climbers, because the weather had improved, and said, 'Come on, we're going to have another go at it.'

But then Mal got sick at Camp Two. So I teamed up with Bob, a Danish climber, and we went up to Camp Three to make our summit attempt. And then I got really, really ill. I was just shaking. I was vomiting. I knew I was getting altitude sickness quite severely. It was like hitting a wall, something had pulled the plug on my energy, there was nothing in the tank any more, I was just completely wasted. On top of that I knew I was a burden to my climbing partner, putting him at risk. As far as I was concerned, enough people had died that year.

That's the only time I actually cried on the whole expedition – when I sat down, tied to a rope about 50 metres below my next camp, and I knew I hadn't got it in me to go on. I thought, 'That's it. The dream's gone. The money's gone. Now what am I going to do?' And I looked up at Bob. He was already up there in his tent and he couldn't hear me. I was shouting to him, but he couldn't hear to come and help me. In any case, I didn't want to bring him back down. I knew that I had to get back down on my own.

It took me nearly four and a half hours to get back down to Camp Two on my own. What would have been a normal forty-five minute descent, turned into a four-and-a-half-hour epic, because I was absolutely shattered. That was probably the most soul-destroying time I have ever known. Knowing that you are walking away, after all the effort and energy you've expended. Everything I'd been working for. I'd been training physically for six or seven months, really, really hard – two or three times a day in the gym. I was physically immensely fit when I left. But all the energy was spent. I thought, 'It's all over.' It's such a dejecting feeling to know it's all gone, all finished.

When I got down to Camp Two, I realised I had a problem with my leg. I crawled into the camp, it was late, it was dark, about seven o'clock, and most of the guys were sealed up in their tents, so at first they didn't realise I'd come back down as I crawled in late. I was on my hands and knees when I got to the tent. Mal and the others hauled me in, got me undressed. They asked how I was feeling. I said, 'I can't feel my left foot. It's really cold.'

'How about your right foot?'

'No, that's fine. It doesn't feel cold.' So they took my left boot off and warmed it up, but didn't bother with my right, because I had said it was fine. But the next day when I woke up in my sleeping bag, I couldn't feel my right leg. I had lost all feeling from my right knee down to my foot. It was just dead. You know when you get 'dead-leg' or a dead arm, and have to wait for the feeling to come back? It was like that, but there were no pins and needles. The feeling never came back. It was like that for months and months. It's still not 100 per cent.

Mal Duff was really good. He said, 'Right. We're out of

here.' And next morning we just bombed off Everest. We got to Base Camp. I could walk on my leg, but I couldn't feel it at all. It's a bizarre feeling. When the feeling didn't come back after a day, I said to Mal, 'I'm going to pack my gear up and make a beeline for Kathmandu, contact the embassy and speak to the medics there.' I thought I might have a blood clot, or some serious problem. As it transpired, well, I'm still alive and kicking!

That March when we had walked into Everest Base Camp, arriving on 1 April, it had taken us ten days. In the middle of June, when we left, I walked out in two-and-a-half days. It was a lot easier because it was downhill, and I was on a mission. I just didn't stop at all. Some of my kit came down on a yak behind me, and I had a Sherpa carrying my gear, and I had a rucksack, and I just hoovered out really quickly, trying to get down as fast as possible.

The first thing I saw when I arrived in Kathmandu was a *Newsweek* magazine, with a massive big spread on the front about the Everest disaster, and huge long interviews with people about it all. I thought, 'I've just come off from there. How can they have got all this detail this fast?' It was huge news by the time I got back down.

The press never bothered me. I never spoke to them. They had got their money's worth of story from the people that had come down prior to us, the story of Rob Hall, Scott Fischer, Beck Weathers and all the accidents, and the sheer disaster of it all. They'd got their stories, and they were just spinning it for all it was worth.

It was almost all the Americans who had given the interviews for the articles in *Newsweek*. There was never any comment or mention of all the other people who had helped, got all the things in place while they were bringing the first people off, and sorted it all out. Nothing about what had really happened.

I did think, 'That's a bit of a cheek.' Some of the stories

I've read, I think 'That's not really true.' But why let the truth get in the way of a good story? I don't think I was peeved. I was just glad to get out of it. I was so shattered, tired and fed up. Everything I'd worked for had gone. If I'd had more energy I might have been more pissed off. But I couldn't get the energy up enough to care. I was jaded and just wanted to get home.

I flew home to London. The people at my old RAF base, Valley, were very good at sorting out medical cover for me when they realised I had a problem. I was met at the airport and taken straight to the National Centre for Neurology and I stayed there for two weeks. I had weighed about thirteen stone when I left for Everest. Now I was under ten stone. I couldn't believe how thin I'd got.

They gave me all sorts of tests – MRI scans, CRI scans, even a lumbar puncture. You name it, I had it. Awful experience – never have one. The worst thing I've ever had is lumbar puncture. Dreadful thing. I suffered for months afterwards from that lumbar puncture.

My biggest concern was to know if I could ever climb again. Or was that me finished? I was a bit scared they were going to cut the leg off. The doctor said it was OK, everything was working OK, I just couldn't feel anything now, but the feeling would slowly come back. I'm still missing a bit of it. I can cut it without realising it. But it's not a major issue.

Back in the UK, the *Edinburgh Evening News* spoke to Mal Duff. He was from Culross, in Fife, not far from my parents' home, maybe about 25 miles from Edinburgh. He got back before me, because I was stuck in hospital in London. The press got hold of him, because Mal was a famous Scottish mountaineer, and his name was bounced around.

So they did a big spread about Mal and what had gone on, and my name popped up here and there. But it was all the death and disaster that everyone wanted to talk about. Unbeknown to us, Mal and I had been officially registered by Reuters as missing for 48 hours, which had caused my mother no end of grief.

The rescue that gave me the most pleasure personally had happened about three weeks earlier, during the week we were ferrying kit and equipment up to Camps One and Two from Base Camp, interspersed with essential rest days. On 19 April I was sitting in my shorts, writing postcards home when one of our Sherpas, Gombo, came into camp and informed us that a Royal Navy diver, 'Ginge' Fullen, was climbing on the icefall and was not at all well. I thought he was probably suffering from a bit of acute mountain sickness – altitude sickness – which a few of the other climbers had already come down with.

I said, 'Where is he?'

And Gombo said, 'He's about half an hour up the mountain.'

I said, 'OK, I'll go up and see if he's all right. You get an oxygen bottle and I'll get one and you can show me.'

I was still in my shorts and T-shirt, because I thought he was only half an hour away. About an hour and a half later we were still climbing up the icefall. What I should have realised was that his 'half an hour' was Sherpa time – because they go like trains – and he had been coming down. Very different from European time, going up. In the end it took us nearly three-and-a-half hours to locate this guy on the glacier. He was still lying on the ground, exactly where they'd left him about four hours earlier. He couldn't move or walk and he had burning pains across his chest. So I gave him morphine. Didn't work. Gave him oxygen. Didn't work. He had a pulse of over 160, which is frighteningly fast. I couldn't leave him there. He couldn't walk. So basically I had to drag him off the icefall and down to Base Camp. It took nearly four and a half hours to get him off. I sent the Sherpa back for more oxygen, because we were running out. People didn't stop to help – they went past us and must have thought, 'He's all right. He's got someone with him.'

Eventually the Sherpa and I between us got him back down and Rob Hall's expedition doctor came to look at him and wired him up and said to me, 'He's had a heart attack.'

This was a twenty-four-year-old bloke, a Royal Navy diver, immensely fit, who had had a heart attack. We got him flown out, and he lived. There was no press interest in that. Nobody writes about that, but that gave me more personal satisfaction even than pulling Lou Kasischke or anybody else off. Because that was just me, going up there and pulling somebody off, when nobody else wanted to know.

I always remember when I first started climbing, thinking, 'If I have an accident, these mountain rescue boys are going to get me out of trouble and bail me out.' And when I found myself in a position when I could actually give something back to the sport that I've enjoyed, I got a lot of satisfaction from it. Helping people. I enjoyed that. I thought, 'Well, the guy's in trouble. Go and give him a hand.' It just seems natural.

You'd be surprised and disappointed to see how a lot of people behave, umming and ahing and going to get a cup of tea. You'd say, 'There's a guy out there in trouble.'

'It's not one of ours, though. Don't bother.'

'He's still a climber. He's in trouble. Let's go and get him.'

They didn't want to know. It was somebody else's problem. Somebody else could go and sort it out. If everybody had that attitude, then we'd all be lumbered.

Lisa: *Do you believe in God?*

Euan: I'm not devoutly religious, but every time I reach a summit, I do sort of ask to be able to get down safely. I don't know why. I'm not at all religious, but I'm not an atheist. It's just not one of those things I've given a huge amount of thought to. Perhaps I'm not one of life's deep thinkers. I don't know. You're asking a lot of searching questions, aren't you?

My mother never knew anything about what had happened until the RADAR People of the Year thing came out. I knew my mother had been worried witless all the time I was up there. The last thing I wanted to do was to regale her with stories of death and destruction and people lost. I knew it had been hard enough for her to cope with the time I was reported missing, believed dead. I'd caused her enough trauma. I just thought, 'Put the whole thing quietly to bed and leave it at that.' Perhaps I should have talked to her about it. I don't know.

I did speak to Dad for about an hour and a half on the telephone from the hospital when I got back. But he didn't go into detail about it with my mother, obviously. I spoke to one or two of my climbing friends a bit about it. I've done a couple of presentations, and I went into print for a mountain rescue magazine. I wrote it all down then. The whole story. A friend of mine, a girl at work, typed and edited for me. I just wrote the whole story down as I saw it. She read it all, and came in sobbing, 'I never knew it was so terrible.'

I'd like to find my original story, because I was angry about what had happened, when I came back. Angry about the way people had reacted. And the way I felt people should have behaved, from other expeditions, and didn't. I went to print about it. And I suppose I was angry because it had all meant I never reached the summit. But getting angry, and writing about it, was probably the start of my healing process.

I didn't know I'd been put forward for an award. When I left the base at Valley, where I had been stationed, they gave me a dinner, all the men, and the station commander stood up and spouted on about all I'd done and how I'd saved people's lives. They were all gobsmacked. They asked me why I hadn't ever said anything. But I felt it wasn't really any of their business. It was my personal business. They hadn't been there. I'd been there. People had died. I just felt it wasn't for public consumption. I'm sure the guys were genuinely interested and wanted to know, and perhaps it was very selfish on my part for not sharing it with them.

I've got no idea how awards are allocated. I know for a fact that if I had reached the summit, I would probably have got a huge gong from the air force, because it would have been a first. But I never even thought about any other kind of award. I had had a nice pat on the back in a report from my boss. I didn't expect anything else.

Once the award was announced, I had my 'famous for fifteen minutes' allocation. I had to phone my mother up and tell her I'd got the award, because the press were round there like a rash. Radar generates a lot of media interest. So my mother said to them, 'What has he actually done?' And they told her the whole spiel. And didn't I get it in the ear that night on the telephone? But she was proud of me, bless her.

Suddenly I was in all the papers. I got some massive stick from the guys at work because of something in the *Daily Telegraph*. It was front-page news in the Scottish papers. I was embarrassed really. They take a little piece of the thing, and they gloss it up. It's probably not factually correct, but they've got to sell newspapers, haven't they?

I enjoyed the award ceremony. It was lovely. I enjoyed it

more for my mother and father. They deserved it more than I did, because they'd gone through hell while I was away. They thoroughly enjoyed the ceremony and meeting Sue Lawley and Moira Stewart, who were lovely to Mum and Dad.

I felt quite humble. Afterwards I thought of things I would like to have said and didn't. By that time Mal Duff was dead. I just wish I'd talked about Mal, who had died that year without fulfilling his dream of getting to the top of Everest. He was a great man. I missed my chance. If it hadn't been for Mal I wouldn't have been there. You never find out from Radar who put your name forward, but I know now it was my station commander at Valley and Mal Duff.

Life has settled down. After three years, I've started to get the urge to go walking and climbing again – it has taken a long time. But at least it's a sign that most of the stress and trauma is over. Normally I would bounce back a lot faster than that. Mountaineering is a passion of mine and I really enjoy it. So for it to have taken so long for me to get the urge to take my boots out and walk in the hills again, that's what made me realise how much of a toll it had taken out of me.

I still think about it occasionally. Sometimes when I'm out on the hills. Or I sit and watch a programme on TV and suddenly it brings it all back. Usually I just think, 'Oh shit, yeah. That was actually quite bad.' I don't know – I think I consciously try to distance myself from it.

It certainly had a disastrous impact on a relationship I was in at the time, which went for a ball of chalk fairly recently, actually. I had been going out with this girl from just before I went to Everest. And it all came to a fairly sad and painful ending about a couple of months ago. It's like they want to share, they want to understand, but they can't, because they weren't there.

Lisa: Yes, I know that from my relationship for five years. The fact that I want to share it with somebody, but nobody saw what I saw, nobody can relate to what happened. I tried to explain things, but through no fault of their own, nobody could relate to it. And so you find yourself distancing yourself from them, because you can't let them in, and then you don't want to let them in. And it is really difficult, isn't it? So then it was all over? Would you say that was from the effects of what happened?

Euan: It's probably too glib to say 'Yes, that experience on Everest was the whole problem.' But it was part of the problem. There are times when you want their help to get over it, and they want to help you, and they want you to talk about it, but they don't understand. You say, 'I can't talk to you, because you just weren't there.' They want you to share something you can't share. It's painful for them and it's painful for you. You know they are suffering, but there's something in you, you don't want to share it with them. So it does impact on your life, there's no question about that.

Lisa: Do you ever cry?

Euan: Perhaps some people deal with stress with tears – but that's usually after the danger is passed. That comes later. You have to have time. When it's all going on, all your mind and energy is focussed on the task in hand. That's part of being a bloke, you can be terribly single-minded, and that gets you through the crisis at the time. How you deal with it afterwards is perhaps what separates the men from the boys. I don't know. All I wanted to do was have a beer.

The only time I cried was when I knew it was all over – for me. I'm not a crying person. No. Seriously. You see a lot of death in the jobs I've done. I've had friends of mine die in aircraft. I've been very close to a lot of violent death, picked up bodies from air crashes and that. You just kind of harden yourself to it. Recently both my grandmothers died and again, I didn't cry. I don't know if that makes me a hard person?

Lisa: Crying is just a form of relief. You deal with it another way. It doesn't make you a hard person. Crying is a release from tension.

Euan: Yeah, that's right. Everybody finds their own way of getting things out of their system.

Lisa: I'm always laughing. That's another way.

Euan: The only time I cried was at the end of the dream. It was soul-destroying. It was something I'd worked personally so hard for. Emotionally you feel a lot more sensitive at altitude. I don't know why.

Lisa: Do you think you are a different person now, from before it all happened?

Euan: I hope not. I hope that fundamentally I'm the same person. Hopefully wiser. I'm certainly more experienced. The mountaineering itself was a huge learning experience. You can't get a better experience of mountaineering than climbing up Everest.

But as a person? I think you probably need to ask my friends to get a better perspective on that. I've always been very relaxed and easy-going. There were times when I became more testy and irritable than I normally am. Whether that was an effect, I really don't know. I think my life is back in balance. It doesn't dominate my life. I don't live and breathe the incident.

It will never leave me completely. It's a mark on my life, it will always be there. It's one of my life's experiences and part of what will mould me into what I am and become later on.

I'd faced death at least twice before, climbing. When you've been so close, knowing that if you don't navigate properly, if you make a mistake . . . and you survive, then it gives you inner confidence. Everything else after that seems unimportant. You know you are in control.

Lisa: Did you find the physical pain harder to deal with than the emotions? Because I think the mental pain is harder to deal with, because nobody can see it. Nobody can understand. Whereas, I can show somebody my physical scars and they go, 'Ffff. That's bad.'

Euan: You're right, and when physical scars heal up they think that's it, it's all over, you're all right now. But sometimes you are not all right. And you do put on a front, when you are talking to people, and to friends. Because you don't want to be seen to be weak. But behind closed doors, you're not over it, and you can be a miserable so-and-so.

Lisa: That's why I called my last book, Behind the Smile *because I was constantly with the media, being smiling and cheerful. But behind it I was pretty stressed out, really. And it did dominate my life for the first two years, which is a long time. And now it's only just starting to stop dominating things so much. I'm now living my life the way I want, doing the things I want to do. But it's amazing how one incident can affect your life for such a long time . . .*

Euan: Yes. You can let it dominate your life. Or you can just accept it and put it behind you. It will mould me –

make me a better or worse person. Then you take it with you, and move on. If you just relive it and relive it, then you never get yourself out of the hole you've dug yourself. I don't know – but I should think that's usually why people get depressed, they dig this huge hole and then can't get out of it.

Fortunately – perhaps I was lucky, and you too – we didn't let it dominate our lives and pull us down. You could be acutely depressed by what's gone on. The inner qualities of life, the injustice of it all, you can't let it get to you.

Lisa: Would you do it again?

Euan: If you'd asked me that six months, a year after I'd come back, would I go back to Everest, my answer would have been 'No'. I didn't have the heart. Basically the heart and soul had been ripped out of me mountaineering wise. But I guess time is a great healer. And now, as you ask me, I would say, 'Yes'. If somebody came up to me and said, 'Here's some money, have another go at it,' no worries. I'd be right back at it. And because of the experience I've got – I wouldn't be worried. Fear of the unknown is the worst thing. But I know what's up there. I know what to expect. I know I've got the skill and the physical stamina to go and do it again. All you need to do is to get fit enough, and get the money together.

But don't tell my mother that – she'll go mad. But I reckon I would have another crack at it now.

Lisa: Are you happy now?

Euan: I can sleep at night. If I had walked away and done nothing, I probably couldn't. Could I have done more? Yeah. I have always felt sad, something has always nagged me, could we have saved Rob Hall? You turn all the options round in your mind. Could we have known where he was and got to him a day earlier? But 'what ifs' don't help anyone. It's self-destructive if you go down that road. Perhaps we could have done more, but we did what we did. It seemed right at the time.

Lisa: (Yawns) Sorry. That was a big yawn. It's nearly two in the morning!

Euan: Oh Lord, now I'm boring Lisa Potts!

Lisa's Reflections

This is a story of endurance over a long period of time, not about a sudden flash of heroism. Euan had time to think about what he was going to do. It was about having to make a choice, having to choose between his own agenda – reaching the summit of Everest – or helping to save lives.

Almost everyone else I met for this book says, 'There wasn't any choice. I just had to do it.' Whereas Euan did have a choice, whether to help or not, and it seems as though there were some people up there who made a different choice.

I think that because of his work in the RAF he does sometimes come across as someone with a wall in front of him. He doesn't cry. He doesn't get upset. He's seen a lot of death and danger before. He's learned to block it out. I think he had blocked out this whole event in a way.

He tells the story, and I actually said to him, 'You tell the story like I tell mine . . . this happened and then that happened. As though it were nothing to do with you.'

He replied, 'I don't know if this is my way of distancing myself from it.'

I think it is. And that's very similar to me. But in my

case, feeling detached is kind of involuntary. It's as though I was unconsciously protecting myself from thinking about it at the beginning, whereas in Euan's case I think it's a deliberate policy to be cool and detached about everything. He's *chosen* not to examine his feelings too much.

In my case, it was self-protection. Everything was pushed down, and it needed to be pushed down. The shock did it. But with Euan, he's learned to do it – perhaps from working in the RAF. But the more we talked, the more he did start to come out about his emotions.

It's a very intense story. Not just what happened to him, but the pain and suffering of so many people that year on Mount Everest. I think it did take great guts and determination to help people down, when he'd set his heart on reaching the summit. He was talking about the frostbite and the way he had a man attached to him, so he had to keep going back up, unhooking the peg, then going back down, then unhooking, and going back up. It must have been exhausting. And he's not a huge guy. And by then he'd really lost a lot of weight so he would have been quite small.

A guy who's got that kind of determination inside them – that's very different from my story. My incident was very quick. But this was over a long period of time, and a lot of thought had gone into it. But he didn't want to make a big deal out of it.

He talks about Rob Hall being up there for all those hours, knowing that he was going to die, and talking to his wife. Euan's way of dealing with his feelings about that was to get out, not to listen to Rob Hall talking to his wife. I know that I would have stayed and listened.

As a person, he's highly organised. He didn't rush about in a panic. And his first instinct after the disaster was to get things organised, find out exactly what the situation was, set up lines of communication. He was definitely needed to do things like that. But the others got a lot more publicity than him. He really is a genuine unsung hero.

His endurance is probably the key word to this story. How he just went on and on and on and on.

When I asked him about religion, he said, 'Perhaps I'm not one of life's deep thinkers.'

It made me wonder. I think I *am* one of life's deep thinkers – but I never was before. A lot of friends say that is one of the ways I have changed. Most of my friends will say that I'm still exactly the same in most ways, except that now I'm . . . One of Life's Deep Thinkers!

Euan talked about his anger. I was glad, because in my own case, I didn't really feel that anger straight away. I haven't felt that anger at all really until quite recently, over the last few months. And my anger is projected onto other things. So when I am angry, it really is to do with what happened to me, but it comes out over other things. Silly little things, usually.

But Euan said that that was his first reaction. He was very angry. He said that his anger was part of his healing process. I'm not sure that I've ever really confronted my anger with the attacker. That's something I've still got to work through. I very rarely think about Horritt Campbell at all. I push him out of my mind. I've only just started to express that anger over the last few months. Little drips. But I think Euan is right – anger is an important part of the healing process.

At the trial the attacker was right next to me. These things make you grow up quickly. Everyone is there. All the press are in the gallery. The jury in front of you. The police are there. The defence. He's in the dock, and you're standing there telling everyone your story – of what he did to you. They gave me the machete to hold in court – the one he attacked me with. He never took his eyes off me.

All those things are very hard. They carve you. That's what Euan said. They carve you into the person you become. He's right.

I've watched myself grow up years and years beyond my age. But in some ways I haven't. In some ways I'm still a little girl, still love to do all the girlie things with my friends. In other ways I think I may have become quite hard. But when you actually see pain and suffering, not just your own, but watch it, like I have in the orphanages I've visited in Rumania and Vietnam, and then someone says they have got a bad cold – I have no sympathy. Before I would have had a lot of sympathy and been kind. Now I just think, 'Gosh, pull yourself together. There are far worse things.' Obviously I don't say it, but I often want to.

I agree very much with Euan, you have got to learn to separate what happened from other parts of your life. It does affect you, but you can't put the blame for everything that happens afterwards on that one experience.

I'm only learning now to separate between the attack and normal life experiences. Most people travel through life learning from lots of little experiences bit by bit, but I had this great big experience which pushed all the little experiences out of focus. So that became the focus. That's why it's only now I've enough distance from it, that I can begin to separate them.

At first I used to think, 'Oh my gosh, everything's going wrong in my life because of the attack.' For the first two years I thought everything was to do with that. I couldn't face getting up in the morning when I went back to work at the school, and I did blame that on the attack, and it probably was the attack. But it was also little things like spilling milk – I would think that was because of the attack, when really it isn't. It's just another life experience.

OK, it took me two years to learn it, but that is something I'm so proud that I've got through. A lot of people spend their life blaming something that happened long ago for everything in their life. And I've learned to separate it. That is not the whole reason for splitting up with your boyfriend or having a row with your mum. Some things will be because of it. Anger. Loss of temper. Shattered nerves which take time to heal. But not everything.

Euan said, 'Life has settled down after three years. I've got the urge to walk and climb mountains again.' That's like me. For a long time I couldn't be with children. But after a certain length of time I started enjoying going back with my Brownies, started being with children, and when they screamed it didn't frighten me so much any more. During the first couple of years I just didn't get the chance to deal with it. But I think even preparing this book has made me realise that it was right to leave it for a bit. Because I've had that two years, and now I am ready to start thinking about these things. It's only now that the healing has really started to happen.

In Euan's case, he has found himself again. After three years, he's rediscovered the desire to pull on his boots and walk in the hills again.

As I've said before, talking to all the people in this book has helped me so much to understand my own experience. And while I was putting it all together, I have had an almost resurrection experience, a bit like Euan's, of rediscovering my old self again. Perhaps not exactly the same person I was before, but a Lisa I hadn't seen since the attack.

I was in the gym a few weeks ago, and I was enjoying myself, and I looked up and I caught a glimpse of myself in the mirror. It was like recognising an old friend. I looked at the reflection and said, 'Hello, Lisa. Where have you been?'